Freed to Obey

Discovering What Galatians Says About Freedom,
Obedience, and Christ's Kingdom

Dr. Christopher Leonard

Scripture quotations marked (BSB) are taken from The Holy Bible, Berean Study Bible, BSB. Copyright ©2016 by Bible Hub. Used by Permission. All Rights Reserved Worldwide.

Scripture quotations marked (ESV) are taken from The ESV® Bible (The Holy Bible, English Standard Version®) copyright © 2001 by Crossway, a publishing ministry of Good News Publishers. ESV® Text Edition: 2011. The ESV® text has been reproduced in cooperation with and by permission of Good News Publishers. Unauthorized reproduction of this publication is prohibited. Used by permission. All rights reserved.

Good News Translation® (Today's English Version, Second Edition). Copyright © 1992 American Bible Society. All rights reserved.

Scripture quotations marked (HCSB) are taken from the Holman Christian Standard Bible®, Copyright © 1999, 2000, 2002, 2003, 2009 by Holman Bible Publishers. Used by permission. Holman Christian Standard Bible®, Holman CSB®, and HCSB® are federally registered trademarks of Holman Bible Publishers.

Scripture quotations marked (KJV) are taken from the King James Bible. Accessed on Bible Gateway. www.BibleGateway.com.

Scripture quotations marked (NASB) are taken from the New American Standard Bible ® (NASB), copyright © 1960, 1962, 1963, 1968, 1971, 1972, 1973, 1975, 1977, 1995 by The Lockman Foundation. Used by permission. www.Lockman.org.

Scripture quotations marked (NIV) are taken from the Holy Bible, New International Version. Copyright © 1973, 1978, 1984, 2011 by Biblica, Inc.® Used by permission. All rights reserved worldwide.

Scripture quotations marked (NKJV) are taken from the New King James Version®. Copyright © 1982 by Thomas Nelson, Inc. Used by permission. All rights reserved.

Scripture quotations marked (NLT) are taken from the Holy Bible, New Living Translation, copyright © 1996, 2004, 2007 by Tyndale House Foundation. Used by permission of Tyndale House Publishers, Inc., Carol Stream, Illinois 60188. All rights reserved.

Sermon To Book
www.sermontobook.com

Freed to Obey / Dr. Christopher Leonard
ISBN-13: 978-1-945793-08-0
ISBN-10: 1-945793-08-2

This book is dedicated to:

My wife, Kris Ann Leonard, whose strength and biblical character have always inspired me;

My father, Wesley Leonard, who always took time to answer my questions about God and His Word;

My mother, Sharon Leonard, who provided my prayer cover.

CONTENTS

Note from the Author

Welcome to *Freed to Obey: Discovering What Galatians Says About Freedom, Obedience, and Christ's Kingdom*! As you'll notice, following each main chapter of this book is a workbook section that includes reflective questions and application-oriented "action steps." These questions and practical steps are meant to help you deepen and apply your understanding of Paul's message about Christ's Kingdom built on faith, obedience, unity, and love.

The workbook sections are included for potential use in independent reflection, group study, discipleship training, or simply discussion with a friend. Feel encouraged to go through these sections with a pen in order to write down your thoughts and record notes in the areas provided.

No matter what led you to pick up this book, I pray that it will encourage you to appreciate the differences among believers while finding freedom in loving obedience to God's commands—to all of His Word—in vibrant faith and unity of purpose with the Body of Christ.

—Dr. Christopher Leonard

INTRODUCTION

A Different Gospel

I am astonished that you are so quickly deserting him who called you in the grace of Christ and are now turning to a different gospel—not that there is another one, but there are some who trouble you and want to distort the gospel of Christ. — **Galatians 1:7 (ESV)**

The New Testament book of Galatians is a letter written by the apostle Paul to the churches he founded in Galatia.

Most people likely think the Gospels were the first books penned in the New Testament but Galatians is actually the oldest. Although it was written in about 50 AD, only twenty years after Christ's resurrection, this powerful book is highly relevant to Christians living in the twenty-first century.

Paul wrote this letter after learning some disturbing news about the gentiles in Galatia who had accepted Christ.

During an earlier visit Paul had told the Galatian believers they did not need to become legally Jewish;

they didn't need to be circumcised to be a part of the Kingdom of God. When Paul found out they were being pressured into doing just that to be a part of the Kingdom, he was not happy. In Galatians 1:7 Paul rebuked the Galatians for believing a different version of the gospel, not the one he taught them.

The word 'gospel' means "good news," but to Paul, this distortion of the gospel was not good news at all. Paul was concerned people were twisting God's truth. He didn't say they were *denying* the truth; they were *distorting* it.

Troublemakers

Who exactly was distorting the gospel? It wasn't the Jews on the outside—unbelievers—who were doing this; it was Jews on the inside. It was Jews who believed in Jesus as Messiah.

Often this issue in Galatians is identified as a problem between Christians and non-Christians. But it's not. It's an internal problem that needs to be dealt with. One term used to identify these people who were preaching a different gospel was "Judaizers," but a better word might be "influencers," or just plain troublemakers. These "Judaizers" were Christians "who adopted Jewish religious practices or sought to influence others to do so."[1]

Paul was dealing with three groups of people found throughout the Scriptures. It is important to know the difference between them, because their differing beliefs are at the center of the whole book of Galatians.

These three groups are mentioned together in Acts 13:26. Paul said to those listening in the synagogue in Antioch, "Brothers, sons of the family of Abraham, and those among you who fear God, to us has been sent the message of this salvation" (Acts 13:26 ESV). Paul's reference to "brothers" (was the converts to Judaism (*ben Avraham*), and to the "sons of the family of Abraham," the Jews. His use of the phrase "those among you who fear God" was a reference to gentile believers, sometimes called God-fearers, who came to the synagogues but hadn't become legally Jewish. These gentile believers were worshiping with the Jews and keeping the Jewish law, but they had not been fully converted to Judaism.

A big debate began to brew. Should gentiles be circumcised and become fully Jewish, or was it okay just to be a God-fearer?

Distorting the Gospel

Many assume Paul was writing about the difference between Jews and Christians and the issue of law versus grace; this is what has been traditionally taught in the church.

Christians have been saved by the grace of God. It's a free gift. It's nothing to do with a person's own efforts. That's great, isn't it? There is no reason to worry about the law God gave Moses, or anything else, because it doesn't apply to New Testament Christians. Isn't that what most Christians think—what they tell new believers?

It's a common conclusion most people jump to when studying Galatians 1:7 because that concept is a part of modern Christian culture. But dig deeper and consider the background: Is that what's going on? Is Paul really talking about law and grace? Making Galatians 1:7 all about law versus grace distorts the entire book of Galatians, and the very thing Paul was fighting against. Notice the strong words Paul used in the very next verse:

> But even if we or an angel from heaven should preach to you a gospel contrary to the one we preached to you, let him be accursed. As we have said before, so now I say again: if anyone is preaching to you a gospel contrary to the one you received, let him be accursed. — **Galatians 1:8–9 (ESV)**

Twice in this one verse Paul said that anyone who preached a gospel against the one he had preached should be "accursed" (Galatians 1:8 ESV). Some versions translate this to say "under a divine curse" (Galatians 1:8 BSB) or "God's curse" (Galatians 1:8 NLT). This was Paul's harsh ruling as an apostle who had received the gospel directly from Jesus Christ. What did the group do that was making trouble? They added to the gospel. They distorted it; they planted seeds of dissension.

Keeping the Law of Moses

Given the severity of Paul's language, it's important we understand what God's "law" is, as discussed in

Paul's letter to the Galatians. In Hebrew the word for 'law' is *torah*. *Torah* doesn't mean 'law' as understood in Western society. Rather, it means God's instruction.

The instructions God gave to Moses and the Israelites—His law—never legally exonerated anyone. That's not the purpose of the law. Paul described this in Romans when he said, "If it had not been for the law, I would not have known sin. For I would not have known what it is to covet if the law had not said, 'You shall not covet'" (Romans 7:7 ESV). According to Paul, the purpose of the law was to show a person what sin was so that he could understand his desperate state and the need to be saved.

Making Galatians 1:7 an issue of law versus grace goes way beyond what Scripture says, because this passage was about one thing: the God-fearers. They were already living with the Jews and keeping the law of Moses. Paul was discussing a certain part of the law, those things that make a person legally Jewish.

Paul said very clearly that they the Galatian believers need not worry about those things. But too often this is interpreted to mean, "You don't need to have anything to do with *any* part of God's law." That's not the same thing at all!

Right from the beginning Paul said the issue was only the difference between becoming legally Jewish and remaining a God-fearer. All three of those groups were already keeping the law of God, so it had nothing to do with obeying *torah*.

Paul said, "There's only one gospel and you guys are distorting it." That means Christians need to be clear about what the true gospel is, doesn't it?

The Kingdom of God

The gospel is defined differently by different people. The term "gospel" comes from the Old Testament and has to do with the Kingdom of God being established on earth among men. That's really what the gospel is.

Most people say the gospel is that Jesus died on the cross to forgive sins and allow people to now go to heaven. Of course that's true, but that is only a tiny part of the picture. In fact, it is a distortion of the fullness of the gospel. Jesus preached more about the Kingdom of God than any other subject. He used the term "Kingdom of God" more than 150 times. He only talked about sin thirty times.

The good news is that God's Kingdom is coming to earth—but most don't see that as the gospel, right? Think how much the gospel has been distorted.

God with Us

People generally don't understand the gospel to be focused on God's Kingdom on earth; rather, the focus is more often on believers going away from this world. But that's the exact opposite of what God says. Jesus said the bad guys will go away, not the good guys: it is the tares (weeds), not the wheat, that are gathered and eliminated first (Matthew 13:24–30). He will establish His

Kingdom on earth for a thousand years. Then He will set things straight.

This is what Israel was looking forward to. Look at their history—the destruction, the devastation, and the persecution—all they had gone through for centuries leading up to the time of the Romans when Paul was writing.

The Jews were looking for God to put things right and for people's sin to be eliminated so He could dwell with them. Sadly, Christians have made it about being pulled out of this world, not being a part of it.

Yet the gospel is God's Kingdom coming to earth. That's what the good news is. "On earth peace, goodwill to men" (Luke 2:14 NKJV). What is that about? It means God came in the person of Jesus Christ to dwell with humanity. God has begun to put things back in order.

Keeping Jesus' Commandments

Just before He was betrayed, crucified, and buried, Jesus said to His disciples, "If you love me, you will keep my commandments" (John 14:15 ESV). He also told them, "Do not think that I have come to abolish the Law or the Prophets; I have not come to abolish them but to fulfill them" (Matthew 5:17 ESV).

Then what does someone who obeys Him have to do? According to Jesus, "let him deny himself and take up his cross and follow me (Matthew 16:24 ESV). It's not a free ride; followers of Jesus are still subject to God's commandments.

So, how in the world could Paul, who was a Jew of Jews—a Pharisee of Pharisees—and said at the end of his life he never veered from keeping the law, then proclaim to the Galatians, "Hey, don't worry about any of that stuff"?

But that's how Paul's letters have been distorted. They have been interpreted to be all about law and grace when that's not what Paul was talking about. This whole debate was about whether people needed to be fully converted to Judaism to be allowed into the Kingdom.

Paul never taught that people don't need to follow the Word of God. Paul was merely imparting to the Galatians, "Don't worry about the Jewish ritual of conversion. God accepts you as gentiles."

Grace and Truth

You can't make Paul a Christian, at least not in the twenty-first-century Western way. He was a Jew who kept God's law his entire life and never told believers to do differently.

But think how big a distortion that becomes when Paul is made into a twenty-first-century Christian who preaches Christians are to live only under grace and not the law. Did Paul say believers live *in* grace? Absolutely, because they do. But he never indicates grace violates the law—*ever*.

In his letter to the Romans Paul explained this further. He wrote, "What shall we say, then? Is the law sinful? Certainly not! ... The law is holy, and the commandment is holy, righteous and good" (Romans 7:7, 12 NIV). And yet in the church today there are many who believe Christians live only by grace and don't need the law.

The Bible says Jesus came "full of grace *and* truth" (John 1:14 ESV). He had both. That's what Paul had, and that's what believers today have: grace and truth.

Paul said distorting the good news changes the message. It is no longer good news at all, because it can lead someone down a road that's not true. As a modern-day Paul, the Christian is responsible for making sure they represent the true gospel and share both sides of the good news—grace and truth—to remain balanced.

Thy Kingdom Come

As the embodiment of grace and truth, Jesus taught constantly about the Kingdom of God on earth. In the one prayer He taught His disciples Jesus instructed them to pray, "Your kingdom come, your will be done, on earth as it is in heaven" (Matthew 6:10 ESV). How heartbreaking that His church teaches to not be concerned about the Kingdom here on earth. Instead, we in the church tend to spend most of our time worrying about getting to heaven!

That's not just a minor distortion is it? That's a major distortion. I'm sure Jesus wouldn't be pleased with this teaching. He wants His followers to teach the truth and to stand on that truth just like He did. Unfortunately, in this generation, standing for truth is often difficult, if not dangerous.

Standing for Truth

What happens to those who stand for what they believe?

In some countries, especially some Moslem countries, Christians are disappearing. In Saudi Arabia more than a million Christians are missing. Some have left. Some have been killed. Some have been put in shallow graves.

Why in the world would a country be against someone establishing an orphanage, for example? Helping their own people? Because they fear the truth.

Followers of Jesus cannot fear the truth. It's like a little kid who gets caught in a lie. Why does the kid lie even when there's no punishment? Because he fears the truth. Because he fears being found out.

Believers can't be like frightened children; they must be people of the truth.

CHAPTER ONE

Christ and the Covenant

Now before faith came, we were held captive under the law, imprisoned until the coming faith would be revealed. So then, the law was our guardian until Christ came, in order that we might be justified by faith. — **Galatians 3:23–24 (ESV)**

I would estimate that 90 percent of people within the church believe the law of Moses has been eliminated. The passages they most likely base this on are Galatians 3:23–24. They believe something similar to this: "I'm under grace, not law. I don't need to keep God's commandments in the Old Testament anymore." However, this is not what the whole council of God teaches—and as followers of Christ, it's imperative to study all the whole of Scripture. Creating a theology based on a verse here and a verse there is will only lead to misinterpretation.

Before diving into Galatians 3:23–23, the key verses for this chapter that will help uncover what Paul was teaching about the law, consider what he said just a few verses earlier in Galatians 2.

Dying to the Law

For through the law I died to the law, so that I might live to God. I have been crucified with Christ. It is no longer I who live, but Christ who lives in me. And the life I now live in the flesh I live by faith in the Son of God, who loved me and gave himself for me. — **Galatians 2:19–20 (ESV)**

Was Paul affirming the law was now void? No. In fact, he taught the exact opposite. These two verses in Galatians 2 demonstrate how Paul upheld Jewish law while recognizing the saving grace of Jesus Christ.

Paul said he "died to the law" that he might "live to God" in Galatians 2:19 (ESV). Some translations say, "live for God" (Galatians 2:19 ESV). Living for God is fairly clear—living a life of submission to God's commandments and loving others—but what does dying to the law mean? Remember, Jesus had said, "I have not come to abolish them but to fulfill them" (Matthew 5:17 NIV). How can Paul die to the law and yet uphold it?

Galatians was probably the first letter Paul wrote, but he expanded on the concepts of Galatians later in Romans. Addressing this issue of abolishing the law Paul wrote:

Is God the God of Jews only? Is he not the God of the Gentiles too? Yes, of Gentiles too, since there is only one God, who will justify the circumcised by faith and the uncircumcised through the same faith. Do we, then, nullify

*the law by this faith? Not at all! Rather, we uphold the
Law.*
— **Romans 3:29–31 (NIV)**

At first read, it might appear that Paul taught these
new followers of Christ that the law was null and void. It
had been annulled and he found no further responsibility
under the law. But was that really what Paul was saying?

The Essence of God

God initiated the law of Moses to protect the poor and
the disenfranchised. That's what the law was written
down to do. This overflowed right from God's heart and
His very essence.

What was Paul saying about the law, then? The law
was not something created only for the Jews or only for
the gentiles. As the essence of God, the law was part of
who God is and who He's created men and women to be.

So Paul was not saying the law doesn't have a
purpose. Rather, the law's purpose was not salvation.
The law was to point a person to their need—and
everyone has need of the Messiah.

Galatians 3:21 asks, "Is the law then contrary to the
promises of God?" Here's the debate that has been part
of the church for hundreds of years: grace versus the law,
or said another way, salvation by faith or by works. Are
these two concepts in contradiction? Firmly Paul
continued, "Certainly not! For if a law had been given
that could give life, then righteousness would indeed be
by the law" (Galatians 3:21 ESV).

A promise says a person will be blessed, no ifs, ands, or buts. There are no conditions to receiving the blessing. Conversely, what does a law say? Mistakes reap consequences. God's promise and His law have different purposes. God's promise doesn't negate God's law because the law's the essence encompasses who God is. The two go together.

The law was meant as a way to guide the entire world to the Messiah. Everything was and is bound up in Him. He demonstrated in life what it was to be the perfect human being because He followed the law. He lived it. And He taught other people to obey it, too.

The Purpose of the Law

In Romans, Paul explained, "Once I was alive apart from the law; but when the commandment came, sin sprang to life and I died. I found the very commandment that was intended to bring life actually brought death. For sin, seizing the opportunity afforded by the commandment, deceived me, and through the commandment put me to death. So then, law is holy and the commandment is holy, righteous and good" (Romans 7:9–12 NIV).

Does it seem weird that Paul said, "I died to the law..." (Galatians 2:19 NIV) and yet at the same time said the law was "holy, righteous and good" (Romans 7:12 NIV). Those phrases don't make any sense if the law has been nullified. But what else could that death mean?

But in showing him his sin the law also condemned him for it, resulting in Paul's spiritual death, "For apart from the law, sin lies dead" (Romans 7:8b ESV). When the law convicts a person, they stand condemned before God—the penalty for sin. Notice Paul's next question: "Why, then, was the law given at all? It was added because of transgressions until the Seed to whom the promise referred had come" (Galatians 3:19 NIV).

If the law cannot save a person, what good is it? This isn't just a rhetorical question, but one Paul has to answer because the natural question for the Jews would be, "Why should we be Jews then? Is there any point if the law can't save us?"

Paul needed to show believers that the law is still crucial without negating the promise because the promise is what saves. This promise was made almost four thousand years ago through a man named Abram (later re-named Abraham). God promised Abraham that the Messiah would come through his seed and every single person in the world would have access to salvation. Don't miss this critical point: salvation was the promise.

But Paul said the law was given *because of transgressions*, or sin. In other words, the law was given as a way of guiding and protecting God's people until the Messiah came—the one through whom the promise would be fulfilled. That is the purpose of the law.

Under Penalty of Death

The law is good, holy and righteous, Paul said. The problem is the penalty—our condemnation. Paul wrote, "All have sinned and fall short of the glory of God" (Romans 3:23 NIV). No one is exempt; all are condemned.

When Adam and Eve sinned in the garden, two things came into being: death and separation from God. Death and separation from God are the punishment for man's sin.

Now turn to another of Paul's letters, Colossians. Paul wrote this letter to the Colossian church during his first imprisonment in Rome. This church had been struggling with some dangerous teachings by false teachers. Combatting this heresy and elevating God's greatness Paul wrote, "And you, who were dead in your trespasses and the uncircumcision of your flesh, God made alive together with him, having forgiven us all our trespasses, by canceling the record of debt that stood against us with its legal demands" (Colossians 2:13–14 ESV).

What did Paul say the Colossian believers were dead to? Certainly it was not their responsibility under the law. Paul would never say that; recall Paul upheld the law. The record of debt had been canceled by God's forgiveness. So in other words, what Paul said believers died to was the *penalty* required by the law.

Till Death Us Do Part

Followers of Jesus died to the just and fair penalty for sin, which was death. Paul explained this concept through the lens of marriage:

> *For a married woman is bound by law to her husband while he lives, but if her husband dies she is released from the law of marriage. Accordingly, she will be called an adulteress if she lives with another man while her husband is alive. But if her husband dies, she is free from that law, and if she marries another man she is not an adulteress.* — *Romans 7:2–3 (ESV)*

As long as a husband and wife are alive, Paul said, they are legally bound to each other; if either one sleeps with someone else they have committed adultery. But what happens if the husband dies? Is the wife still responsible for that contract? No. She is free from the law, and there's no penalty for her if she marries again.

This is not unlike the law of God for the believer. God's perfect law and its penalty separate people from God. Only death can put an end to it—a dead person can't be punished. That's why Paul was able to say, "I died to the law, so that I might live to God" (Galatians 2:19 ESV).

Likewise, a person can't "live to God" when separated from Him. That's why the penalty had to be eliminated, and why Jesus took all the punishment for the world's sin on Himself.

Escaping the Penalty

With Christ's death, for those who believe, the penalty is gone. That's why Paul could praise God that he had died to the law in one sentence but say he lifted up the law as being good, righteous and holy in the next.

This is not an easy concept to understand. Most people read Paul's writings and interpret his teachings to mean they have no responsibility to the law anymore and do not have to do anything.

However, this is far from the truth! There is an unseen war going on between good and evil, and believers are called to fight and not sit back and do nothing. The law and God's instruction are still vital but the penalty for falling short of God's perfect instruction is gone. Every person who has put their faith in Christ will not have to face the penalty for their actions.

That is something worth sacrificing for—worth dying for.

Fully Devoted to God

Many scriptures speak of sacrifice. For example, God proclaimed in 1 Samuel, "To obey is better than sacrifice..." (1 Samuel 15:22 ESV) and "I am sick of your burnt offerings of rams" (Isaiah 1:11 NLT). From the emotion accompanying these verses, it sounds like sacrifices were a horrible thing to God!

However, these words were not about the sacrifice itself. They were about the people who brought the sacrifices. Isaiah reveals the true reason God was upset with Israel's attempts at bringing sacrifices and offerings to Him:

> *These people come near to me with their mouth and honor me with their lips, but their hearts are far from me. Their worship of me is based on merely human rules they have been taught. — **Isaiah 29:13 (NIV)***

The peoples' hearts were damaged. Sacrifices were meant to bring the hearts of the people closer to God but instead they became a set of man-made rules to keep. Jesus echoed Isaiah in the New Testament when He said, "In vain do they worship me, teaching as doctrines the commandments of men" (Matthew 15:9 ESV; see also Mark 7:7 and Colossians 2:22). People too often look at God as the problem, when the problem is often in the hearts of the people.

God is looking for hearts fully devoted to Him (1 Kings 8:61; 2 Chronicles 16:9), men and women who love God with all their heart, soul, mind, and strength. And this does not happen by sitting in a corner and doing nothing.

Loving God wholeheartedly involves deeds—action. It involves works. To be clear, a person is saved by faith alone, according to Paul: "For by grace you have been saved through faith. And this is not your own doing; it is the gift of God" (ESV). However, James (the half-brother of Jesus) also said faith without action is dead faith (James 2:14–26).

Dead works do not care one whit about the person to whom the sacrifice is being brought—in this case, God.

Whether it's money, time, or an activity brought to God as a sacrifice, if it is nothing more than a to-do item checked off the list, it's a "dead work."

But there are live works. There are works that bring life because they are done out of a heart that loves and wants to obey God. That is a whole different matter.

A New Heart

Some people see God as wrathful and harsh in the Old Testament, but see Jesus as the humble Son who came along and fixed it all. Yet, what exactly did Jesus do to the law? Did He make it easier or harder?

It might be surprising to find out Jesus made it harder. He said, "You have heard that it was said, 'You shall not commit adultery.' But I say to you that everyone who looks at a woman with lustful intent has already committed adultery with her in his heart" (Matthew 5:27–28 ESV).

Jesus took the law to a whole new level. He took it from external adjustments of behavior to an internal change of the heart. Followers of Jesus must examine their hearts and analyze what is going inside to make them act a certain way on the outside—and then be willing to allow God to change them according to God's perfect instruction. But Jesus also left believers with His Holy Spirit to help internalize this law.

Lost in Translation

Galatians 3:23 says, "Now before faith came, we were held captive under the law, imprisoned until the coming faith would be revealed" (ESV). The law was put in charge to lead people to Christ that they may be justified by faith.

This scripture may sound a little bit harsh about the law—almost like the law was a bad thing. It made people prisoners. It locked them up with a guard to keep watch. Many people read this and become biased against the law, interpreting it to mean the law was only established to help people come to the Messiah. Now that the Messiah's here, they think, the law must no longer be needed.

Consider, however, the original meaning of some of the words behind this text when interpreting Scripture. The New Testament was first written in Greek, then translated to Latin and eventually to English. Several different translations across many years sometimes leads to interpretation difficulties.

That's likely what is happening in this passage. The original Greek words do not relate to the concepts Paul was talking about.

Walls of Protection

Paul wrote in Galatians 3:23 that before Christ, believers "were placed under guard by the law" (Galatians 2:23 NLT). Typically, prisoners live behind great big walls. They are given meals and allowed periods of exercise but not much else. Guards watch them constantly—indicating the prisoners must have done something terrible to deserve this kind of treatment.

Now picture the walls of ancient Jerusalem. Warring armies often approached from the outside. Were those walls a good thing or a bad thing for Israel? These walls provided security.

The problem with the English translation of "prisoners" is that the original Greek idea behind the word does not imply prison. It is the Greek word *phroureō*, which means "to guard, protect by military guard" or, metaphorically, "to preserve one for the attainment of something."[2] Galatians 3:23 refers to walls of protection, not prison walls.

The Hebrew word for 'law' has an interesting meaning as well. Ancient Hebrew words started as pictures, or pictographs. The Hebrew word for 'law' is a pictograph meaning, "like the fence around life." The Jews understood the meaning behind the word 'law' to indicate walls, but not prison walls. God's law meant protection for their life.

Thus, a more appropriate way to read Galatians 3:23 would be, "We, the Jewish people, were protected by the law, kept inside until faith should be revealed." Understanding the correct meaning behind the word 'law' changes the interpretation dramatically!

The Babysitter

However, in verse 24 Paul says, "So then, the law was our guardian until Christ came, in order that we might be justified by faith" (Galatians 3:24 ESV). That word for 'guardian' in the Greek is *pedagogue*, or in modern English 'teacher.' This is why many people have said the law was like a teacher.

But to understand fully what Paul was saying, it's necessary to look at the original meaning in Greek to see what a pedagogue was. A pedagogue was not a teacher but a household slave in charge of taking kids to school and making sure they returned home safe. Today, a pedagogue would be like a babysitter.

The law was a babysitter!

Paul used this example to show how the law worked and why it was still effective. The law was put in place as protection until the Messiah came to reveal everything the law already said about Him, with perfect clarity.

The Messiah and the Law

Now that the Messiah is here, what becomes of the law? It's not necessary anymore, right? That's the conclusion that most of the church has come to, and to a certain degree it is absolutely true. Now that the penalty of sin has been eliminated, the Messiah is the only teacher needed.

However, the problem is that Jesus (the Teacher) said He did not come to do away with the law. Not only that, but He also proclaimed that not one single letter or penstroke will disappear from the law "until everything is accomplished" (Matthew 5:18 NIV).

Many have wrongly concluded that Jesus abolished the law, since He's now the one believers love and worship with our hearts—but even Jesus said the law can never disappear. Jesus can only say that because the law is part of the essence of who God is, which can never disappear. As long as day is day and night is night, God's nature will never change. And because of this, followers of Jesus should want to obey God's commandments out of love for Him and what He has done.

Taking Jesus Seriously

The law reveals one thing clearly: all people need a savior—Jesus, the Messiah. Once saved, it's important to listen to Jesus and take Him seriously for the entire law of Moses points to Jesus. Paul affirmed this in Colossians 2:17 when he said, "For these rules are only shadows of the reality yet to come. And Christ himself is that reality" (NLT).

Following Christ is not for the faint of heart. Once believing in the life, death, and resurrection of Christ, the next critical step is to study His Word to better understand what He wants. Yes, the penalty of sin is gone, but Jesus is not a lovable marshmallow who allows His people to live however they want; nor is He a genie in a bottle, waiting to answer prayers right away so His people immediately get whatever they want.

Jesus said to the early disciples, "Follow me, and I will make you fishers of men" (Matthew 4:19 ESV). Jesus gathered twelve motley men together and proceeded to teach them the law—His torah. And then He said, "On this rock I will build my church," (Matthew

16:18 ESV), His holy community. This has always been God's plan.

Before Christ, the law protected people; now it is belief and faith in the Messiah that hedges in the believer. This faith does not simply acknowledge who He is, but is a faith that works itself out in obedience to His will. That's the plan.

Crucified with Christ

Look back to Galatians 2:20. Tucked away in this short verse is the single reason Jesus remained obedient to the Father unto death: "For I have been crucified with Christ; it is no longer I who live, but Christ who lives in me. And the life I now live in the flesh I live by faith in the Son of God, who loved me and gave Himself for me" (ESV).

Jesus loved. This was a specific act because Paul wrote using the past tense of the word. He could have said "Jesus *loves* me," but he didn't. He said, "Jesus *loved* me and gave His life for me."

Paul looked at Jesus' life. He saw the sacrifice. He saw what Jesus had done for him. And he realized now that he would live in Jesus. In other words, Paul now appropriated—that is, took on—Jesus' life and His righteousness, because Paul himself was dead and no longer faced the penalty for sin. A dead person can't be pushed!

The Covenant

To understand how in the world Paul could acquire or inherit Jesus' righteousness, it's important to understand the concept of covenant. In *The Lost Secret of the New Covenant*, the English preacher Malcolm Smith explains covenants this way:

> A covenant is a binding, unbreakable obligation between two parties, based on an unconditional love sealed by blood and a sacred oath, that creates a relationship in which each party is bound by specific undertakings on each other's behalf. The parties to the covenant place themselves under the penalty of divine retribution should they later attempt to avoid those undertakings.[3]

Thus, in a covenant, two people or two nations became one. Their destinies were tied together. When one covenant-making partner spoke of the kingdom and of the king, they spoke of themselves as if they possessed everything the king possessed. That is what happens in a covenant.

Paul said he had to die because as long as he was alive, he faced the penalty of his sin. He knew the only way he could do that and keep on living was to appropriate someone else's life. This is what he meant when he said Christ was now living in him. Paul's own fleshly life was gone; following Christ's commands became what typified his life. Everything that was Christ's was now his because of the covenant God extended to humanity through His Son.

This is the status every believer in Jesus has! Who wants to hold on to their old life and the accompanying penalty? Christ calls believers to appropriate His life and to serve Him now with everything they have.

This is done through covenant—the sacrifice He paid for humanity. Believers die and live in Him and for Him—because it's no longer they who live.

WORKBOOK

Chapter 1 Questions

Question: What role should the Old Testament law be playing in your life?

_____

_____

_____

_____

_____

_____

_____

_____

_____

_____

_____

Question: What does it mean for you, personally, to die to sin and take on Christ's righteousness as your own?

_____

_____

_____

_____

_____

_____

_____

_____

_____

_____

_____

Question: What is a first step to devoting yourself more fully to Jesus in your daily life?

_____

_____

_____

_____

_____

_____

_____

_____

_____

_____

_____

Action: Die to the law and to sin through Christ! As you study the Scriptures, recognize the value of the law as a teacher, but above all recognize that Christ paid the penalty for you under the law. Therefore, take Jesus seriously! Devote yourself fully to following Him as you take on His righteousness as your own. Live in Him through God's covenant of the cross.

Chapter 1 Notes

CHAPTER TWO

Freedom in the Law—Salvation in Faith

For freedom Christ has set us free; stand firm therefore, and do not submit again to a yoke of slavery. Look: I, Paul, say to you that if you accept circumcision, Christ will be of no advantage to you. testify again to every man who accepts circumcision that he is obligated to keep the whole law. You are severed from Christ, you who would be justified[a] by the law; you have fallen away from grace. For through the Spirit, by faith, we ourselves eagerly wait for the hope of righteousness. — **Galatians 5:1–5 (ESV)**

Jesus' sacrifice and grace have brought us the possibility of freedom, but freedom means different things to different people. For the politically-minded person, it can mean freedom to exercise one's rights and powers. For the convict behind bars, it can mean release from prison. For a person with an addiction, it can mean overcoming whatever it is that keeps them in bondage. Often, people desperately seek out the idea of freedom as a goal to be attained—something that will solve every problem.

True freedom, however, is much deeper concept. Worldly freedom involves being free from *something*— while biblical freedom is God's divine gift to be free to *do* or *be* something.

The first verse of Galatians 5 says it was "For freedom Christ has set us free; stand firm, therefore, and do not submit to a yoke of slavery" (Galatians 5:1 ESV).

When Jesus died on the cross it brought true freedom to those who follow Him; Paul has much to say about this concept in his letter to the Galatians.

Let My People Go!

Freedom is a concept that comes directly from God; it exists mainly because of Christianity. Many in the Roman Empire were slaves, but *spiritual* slavery ended with Christ.

Most would define freedom as the ability to do whatever one wants whenever they want, and feel however they want to feel. But does this ability to do or think or buy anything one wants truly bring freedom? Actually it has the reverse effect. People caught in this never-ending quest become less free; the more people throw off moral boundaries and protective laws such as the constitution, the more they become bound.

The biblical idea of freedom does not involve total autonomy to do whatever a person wants. It is the freedom to do something specific: to obey and follow God. What did God command Pharaoh to do? "Let my people go, that they may serve me" (Exodus 1:8 ESV). He didn't say, "Let my people go so they can wander around in the wilderness and do whatever they want."

Freedom has to be put within its biblical boundaries or it can't truly be understood. And the biblical boundaries of freedom have always been freedom from the world, sin, and death. True freedom releases people to serve and worship God.

Freedom in the Law

The Jews had a particular way of looking at freedom that can be traced all the way back to the garden of Eden.

Often people's image of the garden of Eden is as a type of paradise where people were free to wander around naked and eat fruit off the trees. But there were boundaries. No one could eat from the Tree of Knowledge of Good and Evil.

Nowadays, laws are regarded as boundaries that curtail freedom. But the Jews perceived the law as what *granted* them their freedom. Don't miss this important fact: God gave the Israelites the law *after* He had brought them out of slavery in Egypt. God's law was meant to protect their new freedom.

Understand this key concept Paul taught in Galatians 5:1. Instead of thinking, "I've been set free so I've got to get rid of that ugly thing called the law that stops me from doing what I want," realize that God's law, His *torah*, was a gift meant to keep His children free.

The Yoke of Slavery

Paul told the Galatians to "Stand firm, then, and do not let yourself be burdened *again* by a yoke of slavery" (Galatians 5:1 NIV, emphasis added). What did Paul mean by the yoke of slavery? Does he mean the law?

One of the most important principles for Bible interpretation is to always consider to whom the author is writing. In Galatians, Paul was writing to gentile believers, not Jews. When he said "we," he was referring to himself and his Jewish brothers; but his message was directed to the gentile Christians.

If Paul was writing to gentiles, how could he be invoking the law? Paul questioned why they were putting on a yoke of slavery again when the gentiles were never under the law to begin with.

Right from the very beginning, sin enslaved humanity. When Adam and Eve sinned in the garden, all people from that point on were separated from the protection of God and became slaves to the powers of this world. Paul wrote in Romans 3:23, "All have sinned and fall short of the glory of God" (ESV). People were no longer able to serve God, now slaves of that system. Paul taught first-century believers they were saved from the yoke of slavery to sin, the same "yoke" from which believers today are saved.

Freedom, however, is living within the boundaries God has set. There's no such thing as absolute freedom, because as created beings all people are subject to the One who created them. Think of how many mothers or fathers have recited this same phrase: "As long as you're in this house, you're going to follow the rules that I set!" Likewise, our heavenly Father expects His children to obey, no matter whether they are Jews or gentiles.

A Waste of Time

The church of Galatia was in fact made up of two different groups of gentiles. One group had decided the only way they could become sons of Abraham—that is, to be saved—was to be fully, legally converted and become Jews. The other group was being pressured to do the same.

Paul had been trying to assure the Galatians they didn't need to become fully converted to be a son of Abraham. Next, in Galatians 5:2, Paul passionately warned the gentile believers groups that if they accepted circumcision, "Christ will be of no advantage to you" (Galatians 5:2 ESV).

The people who wanted to become "fully converted" did not realize they were already a son of Abraham! Paul questioned that if they were going to go through the whole process of being converted and circumcised, what advantage did Christ give them? None.

There's nothing wrong with being circumcised. Paul did not say there was—he was a Jew and he was circumcised! Paul's argument was that doing so brought no benefit. In a sense, Paul said doing those things to become a son of Abraham was a waste of time; gentile believers were already sons of Abraham.

Being circumcised to become legally Jewish in order to be saved was about as useless as campaigning for a job you already have!

Keeping the Whole Law

Paul had already discussed this earlier. Could the law justify a person? Could it legally exonerate them before God? Of course not. The law was never meant to do that. The law was meant to show people where they were wrong, but it was never meant to justify.

This was why Paul continued, "I testify again to every man who receives circumcision, that he is under obligation to keep the whole law" (Galatians 5:3 NASB). What an onerous-sounding statement to our ears! Those who were fully circumcised and converted were responsible for the entire law?

Firstly, however, God and Jesus don't agree that this is a burdensome obligation; rather it is a matter of purpose.

Now what I am commanding you today is not too difficult for you or beyond your reach. — **Deuteronomy 30:11** *(NIV)*

In fact, this is love for God: to keep his commands. And his commands are not burdensome. — *1 John 5:3 (NIV)*

Secondly, Paul's statement in Galatians 5:3 is nothing more than an assertion to gentiles of a Jewish truth. Every single Jew in that day knew they were obligated to the entire law; Paul was simply informing gentiles who weren't aware of this concept.

There's nothing terrible about keeping the law. After all, Jesus said, "If you love Me, you will keep My commandments" (John 14:15 NASB). So it's not such a bad thing, but keeping God's commandments does not save a person.

Justified by Faith

Paul made a statement of fact. He said, "You are severed from Christ, you who would be justified by the law; you have fallen away from grace" in Galatians 5:4 (ESV). Pursuing justification by doing these things misses the point, because the law never justified anyone.

Christ came specifically to deliver all people from sin and through faith to bring those who believe into the family. Counting on entrance into the Kingdom any other way alienates a person from Christ.

"You have fallen away from grace," Paul admonished. I don't think this meant they were no longer saved, but that they missed out on grace. They did not understand that the law could never justify a person because there's no grace in law. This was just a hard fact. And so Paul warned they would miss out on the grace that comes through Christ.

According to Paul, the law would never accomplish the justification the Galatian believers were seeking before God.

And so Paul was able to say in the very next verse, "For through the Spirit, by faith, we ourselves eagerly wait for the hope of righteousness" (Galatians 5:5 ESV). Paul knew the Jewish believers realized the law could never exonerate a person or save them. What could? Only the righteousness found in hope by faith in Jesus Christ.

One Law for Everyone?

We all have only one savior, Jesus. But does God likewise have one law for everyone, or does He deal with different groups of people differently?

Look at the Old Testament and the law. There were laws for men and there were laws for women. There were laws for priests and there were laws for Levites. God gave different laws for different group of people.

He gave the Jews one set of laws and expected them to keep them, but He can give the gentiles another set of laws and expect them to keep those, can't He? That's exactly what He did.

Yes, Paul said, Jewish believers keep the law; they are required to do it—and thus, they do. But justification and becoming adopted sons of Abraham had already happened to the gentiles. The Holy Spirit was in them just as it was within the Jews who believed. The gifts of the Spirit were active in both gentiles and Jews!

Only One Thing Counts

However, Paul told the Galatians that while there are different ways God works with people, there is only one way to be justified. It doesn't matter whether a person is a Jew or gentile, what country they are from, whether they are male or female, slave or free. Only one thing matters, "what matters is faith that works through love" (Galatians 5:5 GNT).

This can sound a bit confusing! On one hand Paul declared it was the law that counted, but on the other, faith was most important. This confusion is rectified by knowing the law and faith were the same thing to Paul. His idea of freedom was that a person would live within the boundaries God set via the law. Faith is not a mere mental acknowledgment of something; according to Paul, faith obeys.

Abraham believed and obeyed. "Now the LORD said to Abram, "Go from your country and your kindred and your father's house to the land that I will show you" (Genesis 12:1 ESV). And Abraham went. He acted. Abraham's faith was more than a mental acknowledgement of something.

Every person who has ever lived is going to stand before God one day in what is called the great white throne judgment. The apostle John wrote about this judgment, saying:

> Then I saw a great white throne and him who was seated on it. From his presence earth and sky fled away, and no place was found for them. And I saw the dead, great and small, standing before the throne, and books were opened. Then another book was opened, which is the book of life. And the dead were judged by what was written in the books, according to what they had done. And the sea gave up the dead who were in it, Death and Hades gave up the dead who were in them, and they were judged, each one of

them, according to what they had done. Then Death and Hades were thrown into the lake of fire. This is the second death, the lake of fire. And if anyone's name was not found written in the book of life, he was thrown into the lake of fire. — **Revelation 20:11–15 (ESV)**

We stand before that great white throne of judgment, what is the one thing that is going to exonerate us? This is the most important thing you will ever know. It's the most important thing you will ever do.

Many will stand before God offering excuses like, "I'm a good person!" And they are going to be made a fool. God's Word has plainly stated the only thing that justifies a man: faith in obedience to Jesus Christ the Lord.

The hardest thing for human beings to do is surrender who they are, but it is the one thing God requires. Submitting to God and believing in the work accomplished through Jesus' death is what justifies a person. This is what it means to love God with all of one's heart, soul, mind, and strength (Matthew 22:37; Mark 12:30; Luke 10:27; see also Deuteronomy 6:5).

I don't know about you, but what will happen at that "great white throne" (Revelation 20:11 ESV) makes me a little nervous. When I am finally in heaven and standing before the great white throne—and every single person who has ever lived is going to stand there—justification is what they will be hoping for. Because without justification there's no hope for any person. Unless Christ declares a person legally exonerated they are in trouble.

I acknowledge the reason it makes me nervous is because I like to stand on my own two feet. I want to come before God and say, "These are all the good things I did!" Unfortunately, all the good effort in the world is not going to work. I could spend the rest of my life worshiping God, praising God, and lifting up His name and never come close to doing enough to satisfy what I owe.

The only way to be confident of one's coming future judgment is to believe what Paul wrote: Have faith in Jesus the Messiah and what He has done! The blessing is available for all to receive.

WORKBOOK

Chapter 2 Questions

Question: How does the law provide freedom? Why doesn't it provide salvation?

_____

_____

_____

_____

_____

_____

_____

_____

_____

_____

Question: When and where have you ever tried looking for salvation in the wrong place?

_____

_____

_____

_____

_____

_____

_____

_____

_____

_____

_____

Question: Where does your salvation come from, exactly?

_____

_____

_____

_____

_____

_____

_____

_____

_____

_____

Action: Don't fall into the convenient trap of disregarding the law or dismissing it as spiritual slavery. Rather, as you read in the Word, remember that the law represents freedom to worship God and a guide to help you avoid slavery to sin and false gods. Yet don't seek salvation through following the law or any set of rules, either. Don't perform good deeds thinking they will save you; rather, find your salvation through faith in Jesus—in His sacrifice and God's grace.

Chapter 2 Notes

CHAPTER THREE

Love and Obey

...just as Abraham 'believed God, and it was counted to him as righteousness'? Know then that it is those of faith who are the sons of Abraham. And the Scripture, foreseeing that God would justify the Gentiles by faith, preached the gospel beforehand to Abraham, saying, "In you shall all the nations be blessed." — **Galatians 3:6–8 (ESV)**

It's never comfortable to overhear people arguing. Often arguments stem from a simple disagreement in what something means.

There is a discussion in Christianity that has been going on as long as the New Testament has existed: the relationship between faith and works. Is believing enough on its own, or do believers need to be doing anything more?

The more we explore the book of Galatians, the more this apparent conflict in Scripture seems to loom large. But in reality, the issue is a simple difference in definition of terms.

Saved by Faith Alone?

Paul said we are "saved through faith. And this is not your own doing; it is the gift of God, not a result of works, so that no one may boast" (Ephesians 2:9 ESV). However, James the half-brother of Jesus and the head of the church at the time said the exact opposite. James proclaimed salvation is not by faith alone; justification comes through obedience to God—faith in action (see James 2:14–26).

Jesus was asked in Luke 10, "What must I do to inherit eternal life?" (Luke 18:18 ESV). And He responded one must keep the commandments; that is, a person must obey God's Word.

So there remains an interesting debate, a debate that has clearly been a part of the church since the time of Jesus. Paul and James seem to be in disagreement. Who is right?

A Question of Definition

Both James in chapter 2 of his letter and Paul here in Galatians 3 use Abraham to defend their position.

Paul said, "Look at Abraham. Abraham believed; he had faith and it was reckoned to him as righteousness." But James came along and said, Look at Abraham. "Abraham believed God, and it was counted to him as righteousness" (Romans 4:3 ESV).

First, it's important to establish a few things—to be in agreement that the Bible is inerrant. If this is true, both James and Paul must be right in what they said.

James said no one is justified just by believing, but rather they are justified by what they do. James' idea of works was obeying the moral Word of God. He saw God's instruction as man's moral direction.

Now, however, look at what Paul said regarding works of the law. Paul defined "works" in a very specific, narrow way. Instead of meaning the whole of the law, Paul focused on those things in the law that make a person Jewish, like circumcision, ceremonial washing, and other conversion rituals—things that brought a person into the covenant. By contrast, Paul also looked back to how a person came into a saving relationship with God prior to Christ.

Salvation in the Old Testament

This line of discussion leads to a common question within the church: If Jesus is the only way to heaven, how were Old Testament saints saved? Obviously, none had ever heard the gospel!

In order for anyone to be saved they first have to be invited into a covenant. Recall that a covenant was a binding agreement with a more powerful authority. God made a covenant with the Israelites promising that through Abraham's seed God would redeem the world— and then God gave them the law through Moses.

Part of the Jewish covenant-making process involved certain requirements. Among other things males had to be circumcised. This was an outward sign of agreement to be under the law. This was why the influencers were saying gentiles couldn't be saved unless they followed all of the law's conditions.

The First Covenant

Paul was a not only a teacher but also a scholar who had spent years studying Jewish history and law. Regarding Old Testament salvation, Paul was insistent followers of Christ understood how salvation happens because Jewish believers suddenly saw gentiles being saved who had never been part of that covenant.

Yes, Paul affirmed gentiles coming in to the fold were saved in the same way as Old Testament people were saved: through a covenant. But Paul looked back much further in the Bible to the very first covenant.

This covenant was made not with Moses but 430 years earlier, with Abraham. Abraham was accepted as righteous and promised blessings (Genesis 17:6–8) *before* God's covenant with the Israelites and the set of laws God gave Moses at that time. Therefore, Paul saw the Abrahamic covenant as a model or precursor to the salvation of the gentiles.

Paul wrote, "And the Scripture, foreseeing that God would justify the gentiles by faith, preached the gospel beforehand to Abraham, saying, "In you shall all the nations be blessed" (Galatians 3:8 ESV). He was directly quoting Genesis 12:3, which says, "I will bless those who bless you, and him who dishonors you I will curse, and in you all the families of the earth shall be blessed" (ESV). The word for 'families' here in the original Hebrew is the word *mishpachah,* which refers to a clan, family or nation.[4] In the Bible, 'nations' is the same word as 'gentiles.'

Therefore, Paul saw the gospel had been proclaimed centuries before Jesus was even born, crucified, or resurrected. It was maybe a bit different back then, but there still was a gospel based on the same promise: that all gentiles will be blessed through Abraham. Abraham was saved because of a covenant based on his belief in God for the promises God set before him, and on Abraham's obedience to Him.

The New Covenant

Thus, salvation has always come to mankind in the same way: through a covenant. Do believers today come through a covenant? Absolutely.

Remember the Last Supper? As Jesus shared the wine He said, "This cup that is poured out for you is the new covenant in my blood" (Luke 22:20 ESV). Followers of Jesus have been invited into a covenant with the Lord, and this is a covenant made through faith that leads to obedience. The Last Supper service was a covenant service setting the standard for how all people would come to faith from that point on: by choosing Jesus to be King and Lord.

In this day and age, it's hard to understand fully what it meant to be subject to a king. And this generation certainly doesn't understand holiness. In order to come into God's presence, there are requirements, just as there were specific requirements for the priesthood in the Old

Testament when approaching God. And one of the first requirements is to understand that God is God.

God is not a human being, and He must not be approached as such. When God gave Moses the law, He set up the proper steps for how to come near Him, and He expected them to remember to prepare themselves this way every time. They were specific, and there were consequences when priests disregarded the proper way.

What Must I Do to Be Saved?

In light of the reverence and obedience toward God we find demonstrated by men and women of faith in Scripture, it amazes me that anyone could believe salvation is by mere mental assent to something we read. But many of us do believe this—because so many of us have been taught to guard against saying that any works have any relevance to our salvation.

To call a person "lord" is to consider the person a master, ruler or other sovereign authority. How consistent would it be to teach a person they can be saved and call on Jesus as "Lord" but not do what He says?

Jesus even addressed this issue. In Matthew 7 He warned His followers many would call on Him as Lord. But Jesus would say, "I never knew you; depart from me, you workers of lawlessness" (Matthew 7:23 ESV). Why? Because they never obeyed. They didn't even care about what Jesus thought. In a sense, Jesus said, *"How dare you call Me Lord and not mean it?"*

When Jesus was asked, "What must I do to be saved?" how did He respond? He said to keep the commandments, and to "Love the Lord your God with all your heart, all your soul, all your strength, and all your mind.' And, 'Love your neighbor as yourself'" (Luke 10:27 NLT). This is an encapsulation of the entire law.

To say salvation is simply mentally acknowledging Jesus is Lord ignores what both Jesus and James said about salvation. And sadly, this is the viewpoint many within church have taken.

I'm convinced the issue of obedience is one of the reasons why the church is not fulfilling what God has designed it to do. Christians are not affecting the world; the world is affecting them because many are not willing to be obedient. They have denied what Jesus and James said in favor of passages like this one in Galatians, on the false premise Paul was talking about obedience to the law rather than obedience to those things that make a person Jewish.

Obedience and the Church

The role of obedience in salvation is as old as Jesus, Paul, and James. It's as old as the New Testament.

Why did James write about works? To clear up a concept people didn't fully understand.

The people who received Paul's letters did not understand he was coming from a Jewish context when he talked about salvation by faith alone. Keep in mind these gentile believers were Greek and did not have the

Jewish mindset, so they misunderstood Paul in the same way many people do today.

It wasn't until Paul wrote about this specific issue of salvation by faith that it became a hot-button issue in the early church. However, Scripture never indicated salvation was by believing without obedience. Obedience is as natural to salvation as anything. Jesus said it, James said it, and Paul said it, too.

As a church, it is a grave mistake to overlook obedience. People are taught they don't have to do anything but believe, perhaps because church leaders fear what would happen to church attendance if people were told right from the beginning that obedience is required. And so believe, but they don't do anything else God says.

Although God's love for us is unconditional, there are still expectations that follow from accepting the covenant He offers us in Jesus. No covenant was ever made that says, "Come in and do whatever you want."

Imagine what blessings might follow if believers did know from the start that obedience is expected! God made it clear there were blessings for obeying and curses for disobeying as part of every covenant, including the new covenant of Jesus. Consider all the parables Jesus told about the Kingdom of God.

The Parable of the Wedding Banquet

Remember the parable of the wedding banquet in Matthew 22:1-10? A certain king threw a banquet and invited all the great people of his kingdom, but none of them bothered to come. So the king sent out his messengers into the kingdom and invited everybody— even the poor and the sick.

At first, it's easy to make an assumption as to what this parable was about. "Wow, look at that! There's no requirements; he invited everyone in."

But then something interesting happened at the end of that parable. Someone walked up to one of the guests and said, "Hey, you don't have the right clothes on. I'm sorry, we're going to have to kick you outside where there's 'weeping and gnashing of teeth'" (Matthew 22:13 ESV).

Was this parable about someone who wasn't well dressed, who didn't have enough money to buy those clothes? No, in those days if one was invited by the king to a banquet, the king provided the clothes. The person who was asked to leave was not obedient and did not to honor the king.

Jesus constantly taught there are requirements for being a part of His covenant and that He alone provides the clothes. Search Scripture to find where Jesus said nothing is required; it can't be found.

As a matter of fact, many readers might be startled about how much He does expect from His children!

Clothed in His Righteousness

Does a person then become righteous through working out their faith in obedience? Let's get this clear: righteousness has nothing to do with what a person does. A place can't be earned at the banquet. Righteousness has to do with honoring Jesus as King and Lord, but not because it's required.

No one gets to go to the banquet unless they are wearing the garments the King has supplied. Revelation 2 tells us this, when John describes his vision of the wedding supper of the Lamb:

> *Let us rejoice and exult and give him the glory, for the marriage of the Lamb has come, and his Bride has made herself ready; it was granted her to clothe herself with fine linen, bright and pure.* — **Revelation 19:7–8 (ESV)**

Jesus provides the right clothes, and those clothes are His righteousness—robes of white. Jesus makes those who believe in Him righteous and the natural response should be to honor Him.

Followers of Jesus are called every day to be obedient out of love for Jesus, who said, "If anyone loves me, he will keep my word" (John 14:23 ESV).

Ultimately, then, our motivation for obedience comes from love, not out of any precondition or legal requirement. Our obedience is to honor Him for what He's done for us, and for the fact that He has made us righteous when we have no business calling ourselves righteous.

One day every person will face God; the Bible says each person's life will be presented to Him like a scroll (Luke 10:20; Revelation 20:12). It will be laid out before Him and be totally exposed, which is never a comfortable thing. Anybody who has worn a hospital gown knows that being exposed is not comfortable.

And yet the Bible says this is what is ahead. The only hope for any person is faith in Christ.

God has the right to pronounce every single person guilty and condemned. But as Paul declared, "There is now therefore no condemnation to those who are in Jesus Christ" (Romans 8:1 ESV).

No condemnation! American pastor, speaker and theological writer Warren Wiersbe says, "The law condemns, but the believer has a new relationship to the law, and therefore he cannot be condemned."[5]

None will be found guilty who are living their life in Christ.

WORKBOOK

Chapter 3 Questions

Question: Where have you encountered the belief that salvation by faith means you just have to agree with certain mental propositions? Why is this understanding of salvation flawed?

_____

_____

_____

_____

_____

_____

_____

_____

_____

_____

_____

Question: What does Abraham's covenant relationship with God teach us?

_____

_____

_____

_____

_____

_____

_____

_____

_____

_____

_____

_____

Question: What must you do to live out your faith in obedience? What is required of you?

_____

_____

_____

_____

_____

_____

_____

_____

_____

_____

Action: Don't let anyone convince you that faith is a mere matter of mental agreement with certain ideas or doctrines. You must live out your faith! Therefore, follow God's commandments and obey His Word, but do so out of love for Him, not to try to earn your salvation or become someone you're not. Remember the fundamental importance of faith and faithful obedience, rather than ritual, to God's original covenant with Abraham. If you wish to be saved, you must accept Christ and His sacrifice, and clothe yourself in His righteousness.

Chapter 3 Notes

CHAPTER FOUR

How to Live by Faith

What then shall we say was gained by Abraham, our forefather according to the flesh? For if Abraham was justified by works, he has something to boast about, but not before God. For what does the Scripture say? "Abraham believed God, and it was counted to him as righteousness.
— *Romans 4:1–3 (ESV)*

American writer, entrepreneur, and publisher Mark Twain was most likely not a follower of Christ, instead placing his "faith" in salvation by works as the following anecdote suggests:

The story is told of a businessman well known for his ruthlessness who announced to Twain that "Before I die I mean to make a pilgrimage to the Holy Land. I will climb Mount Sinai and read the 10 Commandments aloud at the top." Twain replied "I have a better idea. You could stay in Boston and keep them."[6]

Twain believed the lie that the Ten Commandments can actually be kept, in the concept of salvation by works. Though human beings are hard-wired to want to do everything themselves—even save themselves—God knows this is not only impossible but also it is not His best. He respects His children enough to say, "I think you can realize that living this way in a love relationship with Me is far better than man's way of trying to earn salvation." In Romans 4, Paul points back to where this promise of salvation through faith began.

A New Relationship

Scripture tells us, "He [God] will not leave you or forsake you" (Deuteronomy 31:6 ESV). How can those who are etched on the palm of His hand ever be separated from Him? Who's strong enough to take a person out of the hand of God? These promises should be so motivating to believers they should want to put all their resources and thanksgiving into keeping His Word.

God wanted to establish a new relationship with His people. That's why He gave the Holy Spirit in the first place—so that followers of Jesus could live in this new way.

God's Three-Point Plan

God's plan for mankind can be summed up in three stages. These stages are revealed in the Old Testament, through the establishment of His people Israel as a nation.

Step One: God wants to save. The first thing God did to reveal Himself as Redeemer was not through the giving of the law at Sinai, but rescuing Israel out of slavery in Egypt. He took His treasured possession from being slaves to someone else and transferred ownership to Himself. That is the very first thing God wants to do for believers, too. He revealed His heart for His people most completely in offering His Son. John wrote of this gift, "For God so loved the world that He gave His only begotten Son, that whoever believes in Him should not perish but have everlasting life" (John 3:16 NKJV). God wants to save people.

Step Two: God wants to gather His people together. After bringing the children of Israel out of Egypt, God gathered them. He called them together at the foot of the mountain and said, "I want you to be a separate group of people. You are My people." God is always looking for His people, and wants to gather His people together.

Step Three: Be holy. When God called His people together at the foot of the mountain He said to them, "You shall be holy to me, for I the LORD am holy and have separated you from the peoples, that you should be mine" (Leviticus 20:26 ESV).

God saves them, He gathers them, and He seeks to make them holy. Now there might seem to be a little bit of a problem with that word 'holy' as many people think, "I can't be perfect like God is perfect, so I give up."

But to be holy doesn't mean to be perfect.

Yes, God is perfect. But to be holy means to be set apart for God and His chosen purpose. That's what God wants to do. He called the Israelites to the mountain and then proceeded to tell them what a holy people looks like. They love one another. They forgive one another. They bear one another's burdens. They look for the best in others.

Those steps all come from the Old Testament because that has always been God's plan: to save, to gather His people together and to make them holy. So, it can be said that another purpose of the law was to reveal what a holy, set-apart people should look like.

The natural next step for people who have been saved and called together should be to be holy as God is holy. And the law reveals how.

What Is Real Faith?

Living a life of holiness leads right back to the issue of faith—and the natural tendency to want to discard God's law. But Paul said to live by faith means loving God and desiring to obey Him. It means longing for God's blessings that come with obedience. It doesn't matter if a person is a Jew or a gentile, a man or woman, slave or freeman.

Real faith requires a full-time, faithful relationship with God. It's nothing that can ever become institutionalized. If it does, it's over. That's why the church is not an organization, it's an organism. It's alive, moving and active. And it has a Head who is able to direct, speak and move God's people. It's a real relationship through faith.

The law in itself is not based on faith. What is faith? Obedience to God. Always hearing from God. Always obeying God, no matter what He tells you.

Faith, real faith, can never be just about the law. Real faith is full-time listening to God—someone who's a person, but a living God. "For the word of God is living and active, sharper than a two-edged sword..." (Hebrews 4:12 ESV). That's the kind of God Paul wants those to whom he is writing to understand.

It can be hard to worship God like that. Human beings are creatures of habit who like routines and rituals. Many are checklist people who keep a running list of things to do and love it when something is moved off their plate.

Isn't this how people are with faith sometimes? It sounds much easier to simply check things off with God instead of taking the time to be with Him, talk with Him and love Him with all of one's heart, soul, mind, and strength.

But loving God in this way is not a ritual, nor even a religion. This kind of love only comes in a relationship.

Chapter 4 Questions

Question: What is the first step in God's three-point plan for humanity? What is your role? What are your responsibilities?

_____

_____

_____

_____

_____

_____

_____

_____

_____

_____

_____

Question: What is the second step in God's three-point plan for humanity? What role and responsibilities do you have in this step?

_____

_____

_____

_____

_____

_____

_____

_____

_____

_____

_____

_____

Question: What is the third step in God's three-point plan for humanity? What are your relevant role and responsibilities?

_____

_____

_____

_____

_____

_____

_____

_____

_____

_____

Action: Let God save you—because He wants to! To live a life of faith, embrace your role in His master plan: accept the salvation He offers in Christ, unite with other believers, and be holy. Individually and collectively, break free from the grip of ritual on your heart and mind. Don't think you can be perfect through your own power or abilities, or through the law or any particular formula. Rather, through attentiveness and obedience to His Word, keep yourself set apart for His purposes and a real, devoted relationship with Him.

Chapter 4 Notes

CHAPTER FIVE

Perfect Redemption

*Christ redeemed us from the curse of the law by becoming a curse for us—for it is written, "Cursed is everyone who is hanged on a tree." — **Galatians 3:13 (ESV)***

When I was a teenager; I had a good friend who was my youth leader.

This guy was really committed to us as teenagers. He would leave his house open and let us barge into his life whenever we wanted to. He was always available if I was having girl problems or had a spiritual question. He was also a master mechanic. When you're young you have cars that fall apart regularly, that's a plus in a friendship! I would drag my wreckage over to his house and he would fix it up and send me back out until the next time.

He was someone that I really looked up to, because he showed that he cared about me. His name was Milt Schultz, and to this day there is not one single thing that

I would not do for him, because that's the kind of guy he was for me.

A Transfer of Ownership

Redemption is an oft misunderstood concept, but when understood correctly should have the same effect on believers that my friend had on me. Jesus has redeemed mankind, and when a person understands just how much God has done for them they will desire do anything in return for Him. They will be available twenty-four hours a day for His commands.

Paul continued in his letter to the Galatians "Christ redeemed us from the curse of the law by becoming a curse for us— for it is written, 'Cursed is everyone who is hanged on a tree'" (Galatians 3:13 ESV).

How often do churches swell with music adorned with lyrics about Christ as the "Redeemer"? That word (like hundreds of others) has become so common among believers it falls in the "Christian-ese" category. But what does the word 'redeemed' mean?

To redeem means "to buy back" or "to ransom."[7] It is a word tracing meaning from the world of slavery. A slave would be put up on the auction block; people would bid on him and the price would be paid. What happened then? Ownership and authority over that slave was transferred to the new owner.

That's the real meaning of biblical redemption. Often people define redemption in terms of a slave being freed—and as believers, correlate that to being freed in

Christ. But redemption is not about freedom; it's a transfer of ownership.

The Balance Sheet

The next question to be asked is: What are believers transferred from?

In the Old Testament the covenant was full of promises of blessings for obeying the law, and warnings about the curses that would happen for disobedience—what Paul calls "the curse of the law" in Galatians 3:13 (NIV).

Think in terms of profit and loss columns in a balance sheet. Good accounting results in the "loss" column being wiped out.

Paul said to receive blessings there has to be a way to rid oneself of the curses—because a believer can't have both. And there's no such thing as an eraser for a book like God has. It has to be erased by God Himself. And that's what Jesus has done. Galatians 3:13 says, "Christ redeemed us from the curse of the law" (NIV).

Perhaps people don't understand the depths of what Jesus has done for them. It's far more than freeing people from death. The whole "loss" column is about the curses that will happen if a person doesn't obey.

The Curse of the Tree

In the second part of Galatians 3:13 Paul said, "Cursed is everyone who is hanged on a tree" (ESV). Why would Paul bring that up? That argument was commonly used in the first century by the Jews who would say, "Jesus cannot possibly be the Messiah. And I can prove it, because it says in Deuteronomy 21: 23, 'a hanged man is cursed by God.' And Jesus was hanged on a tree."

But circle back and read that passage in Deuteronomy. What the Scripture really says is if a man is guilty of a capital offense and is put to death and hung on a tree, "his body shall not remain all night on tree, but you shall bury him the same day, for a hanged man is cursed by God" (Deuteronomy 21:23 ESV).

Jewish scholars typically forget the part about a person guilty of a capital offense. Jesus doesn't fall into that category, does He? What offense was He crucified for?

When someone was crucified a sign was hung around their neck stating their crime. "Do not write, 'The King of the Jews,' but rather, 'This man said, I am King of the Jews'" (John 19:21 ESV). The sign around Jesus' neck said He was king of the Jews. The Jews didn't like that. They said, "Why don't you say 'He said He was the king of the Jews'?" However, Pilate said to leave the sign alone, so Jesus died with His royal rank proclaimed for all to see. But Jesus wasn't crucified for a capital offense.

Paul takes that argument and turns it up on its head. He said Jesus became a curse to erase *the* curse.

Recall how redemption works: someone is paid off so that a debt or curse is removed. Jesus became a curse so that His people didn't have to suffer those curses.

Crowned with Steadfast Love

I always like to ask the "why" question. Why did Christ suffer and redeem us? What possible reason could He have for that? The next verse in Galatians 3 reveals two things. It says Jesus redeemed His people so that "the blessing of Abraham might come to the Gentiles, so that we might receive the promised Spirit through faith" (Galatians 3:14 ESV).

First, Jesus redeemed humanity so that all the blessings—all the good things that God has in mind—would be extended to all people, gentiles included. Those blessings can be found in Psalm 103. Let's look at just a few verses:

Bless the LORD, O my soul, and all that is within me bless his holy name! Bless the LORD, O my soul, and forget not all his benefits [or forget not His blessings], who forgives all your iniquity, who heals all your diseases, who redeems your life from the pit, who crowns you with steadfast love and mercy. — ***Psalm 103:1–4 (ESV)***

That word translated as 'steadfast love' is the Hebrew word c*heced*, which is the word for God's faithful covenant love.[8] It's a rock-solid agreement to give a person love and mercy. God had crowned his people with this kind of faithful love.

Paul declared that God had redeemed His people so that the blessings that were promised in Scripture to Israel could now come to the gentiles. That is an amazing thing! Jesus took the penalty that all human beings owed—one that they would never be able to pay—and erased it so that they could receive the blessings.

What kind of a person would do that? Certainly not a human being, because if a person holds something against their brother they tend to write those in stone and go over them and rehearse them in their minds thinking, "That person is going to pay for that if I'm ever going to forgive them."

God didn't do that. He wanted so badly to give His people the good things, He sent His Son to remove the penalty for disobedience from the balance sheet.

Written on Our Hearts

The second reason why He redeemed humanity is also found in Galatians 3:14. Jesus redeemed all people once so that they could receive the blessing, but also "so that by faith we might receive the promise of the Spirit" (NIV). Now what does that mean?

Though many believe this to be the promise that the Spirit is coming, that is only the surface level interpretation. What was the Spirit promised for?

Take a look at Jeremiah 31:33. It says, "For this is the covenant that I will make with the house of Israel in those days, declares the LORD: I will put my law within them, and I will write it in on their hearts. And I will be their God, and they will be my people" (ESV).

So what did God promise the Holy Spirit would come and do? Eliminate the law? No, not to eliminate it, but to write it on people's hearts. The Holy Spirit's role is to free people up from the negative column of curses so that they can enjoy all the blessings of God, and help God's people keep the law of God within them.

Both of these things are why people have been redeemed. They have been redeemed because God would rather His children have blessings than curses. And they've been redeemed so they might be the dwelling of the Holy Spirit and have Him in action in their lives, so that each person can be gifted in a different area to serve the church.

Gifts in the Church

Gifts are normally about getting something. But God's kind of gifts are different because these gifts are given to be used to serve one another.

No gift functions on its own. That's why if a person says to themselves, "I can best worship outdoors in nature. I just don't need this whole church thing," they have just taken the gift of God and slapped Him in the face with it. This is as good as saying "I'm not going to use it," because that gift will not function unless it is used in conjunction with the people of God.

God does not give a person a gift to better serve them; it is to serve the people around them. That's how the Body functions. That's why the church is described as the Body of Christ, because every person plays a different part doing different things.

Sometimes, however, while using certain gifts a person might look over at the other parts and long to be able to do what the other person is doing. Instead of embracing the unique gift God has given for service on this earth, comparison begins.

God gifts the Body so that nothing is lacking, but each person has the ability to choose whether or not to do those things that God has asked them to do. God is not a slave master.

The Point of Redemption

You have been redeemed from slavery, but that doesn't lessen any of God's Word—His instructions as to what each child of God should be doing. It just takes the penalty out of the equation. And how many are able to function much better knowing the penalty is off the table? It's like a kid hearing his mother warn, "Wait till your father gets home!" When I was a young boy, that wrecked the rest of my day. I would hide in the shadows, looking for ways to explain my way out of trouble.

The penalty for sin is now gone, and believers have a Redeemer who has done everything, including surrendering His own life, so that they can embrace all of the blessing without the curse.

The idea of a savior hanging on a tree was a stumbling block for the Jews. Paul said in 1 Corinthians 1:23, "But we preach Christ crucified: a stumbling block to Jews and foolishness to Gentiles" (NIV).

But here in Galatians 3, Paul takes that argument and turns it on its head. Yes, maybe Jesus was cursed to hang on a tree, but look what He redeemed in the process. He *became* a curse so that no person would have to bear the brunt of the curse.

The whole point of redemption is so that you realize all the good that's going to come to you now because of what He's redeemed you from. He has good plans for you, not plans to harm you. The proof is what He did.

The book of Ruth offers a beautiful picture of redemption, as well as inclusion of gentiles to all of the Abrahamic promises. Ruth, a Moabite gentile, married a Hebrew man who tragically died. Following her Jewish mother-in-law Naomi back to Israel, Ruth went to gather barley in the fields. Boaz, a near kinsman to Naomi, assumed responsibility for Ruth joining her in marriage.

Scripture refers to Boaz as Ruth's "kinsman redeemer." Boaz bought the responsibility to care for both Naomi and Ruth, but also the right to marry Ruth, a foreigner. Subsequently, Ruth received all of the blessings of an Israelite.

In the same way, Jesus redeemed mankind from the bondage of sin and for freedom in Him. Those who believe receive all of the promises of Israel. What *checed* loving-kindness!

Understanding all of this, it's easy to see how followers of Jesus want to treat Him the way I treated my friend at the beginning of the chapter. There's not one single thing that I wouldn't do for God now. There's not any law that's too crazy. Why? Because I love God. I love Him for all that He's done.

Nothing from God should be too much of a request. Believers should always be ready to love and honor God for what He has done; that's what redemption really means.

WORKBOOK

Chapter 5 Questions

Question: What's on your spiritual balance sheet? What is in your profit and loss columns, respectively? How or where does Christ appear on your balance sheet?

_____

_____

_____

_____

_____

_____

_____

_____

_____

_____

_____

_____

Question: How does following the Holy Spirit work in practice? How does He help and guide you on a daily basis?

_____

_____

_____

_____

_____

_____

_____

_____

_____

_____

_____

_____

Question: What are your gifts? How has the Spirit led you to use them? How might He lead you in this regard?

_____

_____

_____

_____

_____

_____

_____

_____

_____

_____

_____

Action: Let God redeem you by allowing Christ and the Holy Spirit to wipe the sin from your balance sheet.

Then let the Holy Spirit guide you in applying and living out God's Word daily, and in embracing and using the particular gifts with which He blesses you. Pray that the Spirit will guide you in using your gifts for His purposes, without concerning yourself about others' spiritual gifts. In love, devote yourself to your new owner, God, who redeemed you, rather than to your old master, sin.

Chapter 5 Notes

CHAPTER SIX

Living by the Spirit

You were running a good race. Who cut in on you to keep you from obeying the truth? That kind of persuasion does not come from the one who calls you. A little yeast works through the whole batch of dough. I am confident in the Lord that you will take no other view. The one who is throwing you into confusion, whoever that may be, will have to pay the penalty. Brothers and sisters, if I am still preaching circumcision, why am I still being persecuted? In that case, the offense of the cross has been abolished. As for those agitators, I wish they would go the whole way and emasculate themselves!

You, my brothers and sisters, were called to be free. But do not use your freedom to indulge the flesh; rather, serve one another humbly in love. For the entire law is fulfilled in keeping this one command: Love your neighbor as yourself." If you bite and devour each other, watch out or you will be destroyed by each other.

So I say, walk by the Spirit, and you will not gratify the desires of the flesh. For the flesh desires what is contrary to the Spirit, and the Spirit what is contrary to the flesh. They are in conflict with each other, so that you are not to do whatever you want. But if you are led by the Spirit, you are not under the law.

The acts of the flesh are obvious: sexual immorality, impurity and debauchery; idolatry and witchcraft; hatred, discord, jealousy, fits of rage, selfish ambition, dissensions, factions and envy; drunkenness, orgies, and the like. I warn you, as I did before, that those who live like this will not inherit the kingdom of God. **— Galatians 5:7–21 (NIV)**

Back in 2013, a pastry chef with a damaged knee, Tam Chua Puh, confessed he took a short cut in a marathon. The result? Tam was the first Singaporean to cross the finish line. Unfortunately, he had only run 6 kilometers of the 42-kilometer route, winning the race but offending marathoners who had been passed up (and who had run the whole thing). Come to find out, Tam only wanted the race T-shirt.[9]

In Galatians 5:7, Paul said, "Who cut in on you to keep you from obeying the truth?" Paul used imagery of a race—and like Tam, who took the medal for winning without earning it—wants to know who was "cutting in" on the Galatians. However, in Paul's metaphor, He was referring to false teachers.

Remember, Paul was talking to groups of gentiles—especially to the group of God-fearers—because they were the ones who wrote him first. Recall these God-fearers had believed they didn't need to be converted, but were being harassed by people who were telling them the opposite.

Going Around in Circles

In response, Paul harshly rebuked the Galatians. It was as if he said, "What's wrong with you? You were running such a good race; you were on fire for God. You didn't care about all of this external stuff. You were running full tilt in the direction that God wanted you to go, but then somebody cut in on you."

Sometimes while driving I will have a moment of questioning where I think, "Am I going in the right direction?" I immediately slow down. I go around the block again and again, not sure if I'm on the right road or highway.

That's what Paul implied. The Galatians were going in the right direction and doing what God wanted them to do when a false teacher cut in on them and told them they were going down the wrong path. Their momentum was slowed and they were distracted.

One can sense from Paul's wording how frustrated and even angry he had become because his desire was God's desire—to see believers go forward, not around in circles.

The Yeast in the Dough

Then in Galatians 3:9 Paul compared this negative influence to a little bit of yeast working through a batch of dough. A tiny bit of yeast can magically spread throughout an entire dense lump causing the dough to rise and become a loaf of bread.

Problems within the church, for example, often begin when somebody—one person—becomes upset and starts to spread rumors and gain people for his side.

One person who's upset can infect the whole church. I've seen many church splits that have started that way.

It has been over what hymnal should be used, what kind of songs should be sung, and even what kind of clothes church members should be allowed to wear. It never has had anything to do with theology. That's what Paul said these "false teachers" did.

The Offense of the Cross

> Paul continued: "But if I, brothers, still preach circumcision, why am I still being persecuted? In that case the offense of the cross has been removed." — **Galatians 5:11 (ESV)**

When Paul refers to "the offense of the cross" to the Jews, could he mean their frustration over being asked to accept that the Messiah had died? Not likely. More probable was that the Jews were upset because the gentiles were being told they were now sons of Abraham without converting, something many Jews could not tolerate. If the circumcision issue could have been dropped, there would have been no offense; but Paul was not willing to let that go because there was important truth he knew the Galatians needed to embrace.

In fact, he felt so strongly about this his exasperation comes through clearly in Galatians 5:12. In the New International Version Paul called them "agitators" and said, "I wish they would go the whole way and emasculate themselves!" (NIV). That is, Paul was stirred to such passion that he suggested anyone wholly convinced of the redemptive value of circumcision should practice what they preached and finish the job by self-castration. Strong words, indeed!

Free, But...

Thus, Paul finally put to rest the issue that one does not have to be circumcised to become part of the Kingdom of God—part of the family. Salvation had nothing to do with circumcision. Not missing a beat, Paul continued: If the gentiles were not responsible for keeping the law the same way the Jews were, what were gentiles responsible for?

In verse 13 he said, "My brothers and sisters, were called to be free. But do not use your freedom to indulge the flesh; rather, serve one another humbly in love" (NIV)

Every time a verse in Scripture says God's people are free, what comes next? The boundaries.

Total freedom is a myth. It doesn't happen. Even when fledgling America fought the War of Independence, it was freed from Britain but became responsible to state and federal governments within the United States. There is no such thing as doing whatever one wants.

Love Your Neighbor

God freed humanity from sin and death so that His people could serve Him. Galatians 5:14 summaries what is now required of the believer: "For the whole law can be summed up in this one command: "Love your neighbor as yourself"" (Galatians 5:14 NLT).

What Paul said in effect was, "You are freed from the law, but out of love, still responsible to the law." Loving others is a summary of the entire law.

Paul warned these two groups of people that if they were not careful, they would destroy each other by putting too much focus on differences.

Unfortunately, the very thing Paul warned the Galatians about is happening today. A church finds a kind of difference with somebody and forms another denomination. People bite and devour and churches split. Where's the love in that?

Supernatural Motivation

There is a spiritual war going on, not only within churches but also inside every person. How God wants His people to function is in direct conflict with the world and man's sinful nature.

> But I say, walk by the Spirit, and you will not gratify the desires of the flesh. For the desires of the flesh are against the Spirit, and the desires of the Spirit are against the flesh, for these are opposed to each other, to keep you from doing the things you want to do. — *Galatians 5:16–17 (ESV)*

Paul seemed to jump from discussing love to a new topic: the Holy Spirit. Contrary to what many people in the church might believe, the Holy Spirit does not show up for the first time in the New Testament. In fact, there are many times in the Old Testament where Scripture indicates God's Spirit was active and present and would be revealed in a new way at some point in the future.

The prophet Ezekiel revealed why God would one day send His Spirit—hinting at the pouring out of God's Spirit at Pentecost after Jesus' ascended to heaven:

> *I will give you a new heart, and a new spirit I will put within you. And I will remove from the heart of stone from your flesh and give you a heart of flesh. And I will put my Spirit within you, and cause you to walk in my statutes and be careful to obey my rules. — **Ezekiel 36:26–27 (ESV)***

The Holy Spirit's function within the believer would be to provide supernatural motivation to love God so much that they would want to keep His Word. Jesus said, "I will ask the Father, and He will give you another Counselor to be with you forever" (John 14:16 HCSB), another one who's been acting the way Jesus had. True to His Word, Acts 2 reveals fifty days after Jesus ascended to heaven, God's Spirit descended to dwell within everyone who would call on the name of Jesus.

The Work of the Spirit

Not once did Jesus differ or invalidate something that His Father said. He only fulfilled what God said in His Word. In the same way, the Spirit of God will never invalidate either the Word of the Son or the Word of the Father. It's impossible because the Father and the Son are one. Jesus affirmed this in John 10:30 when He said, "I and the Father are one" (John 10:30 ESV).

Believers often try to separate Jesus from the Father, quoting Galatians 5:18 as support: "If you are led by the Spirit you are not under the law" (Galatians 5:18 ESV). The thought process is, "Well, I've got the Spirit. I don't need to look at the Old Testament anymore. I don't need to study the law. I don't need to read the Word of God because I've got the Spirit."

A pastor friend of mine believed this so strongly that when it came to studying for his sermons he said, "I don't need to study the Word of God. I'm just going to let the Spirit talk."

The problem is the Spirit is never going to differ from the Word of God or anything that Jesus said, a truth oft forgotten. Yes, the Spirit indwells believers and gives guidance and direction, and even convicts. But Paul taught that the work of the Spirit is a higher principle. The Galatian believers were still required, as anyone believer would be, to keep the Word of God.

However, followers of Jesus possess something new that is far greater; the Spirit takes believers to a whole other level.

The List of Rules

By contrast, the Jews were used to living life according to a checklist: do what the law says, and check it off.

My father used to head out to work and leave a list of chores for me as a child: mow the lawn, do the gardening and so on. He would come often home to find those chores weren't done because I didn't feel like doing them. He had a problem with that. Go figure. "You don't feel like it? I'll show you what you're going to feel," he would rebuke!

All the law can do is provide a bunch of rules. Most human beings can't get excited about that! What can the Spirit do beyond that the law?

Galatians 3:19 says, "Now the works of the flesh are evident: sexual immorality, impurity, sensuality, idolatry, sorcery, enmity, strife, jealousy, fits of anger, rivalries, dissensions, divisions, envy, drunkenness, orgies and things like these" (ESV).

It's almost as people think, "Okay, I'll just put that on my refrigerator and try not to do those things." Guess what? Every single one of those sin issues comes from Old Testament law.

Paul knew the gentiles hadn't been raised with the Old Testament law, but he also knew the acts of the sinful nature were obvious. Those sins were moral issues. And so Paul listed them and said, "I warn you, as I warned you before, that those who do such things will not inherit the Kingdom of God" (Galatians 5:21 ESV).

Once he identified this list of moral sins, Paul continued on to discuss the difference between the law and the Spirit in terms of what he called the "fruit of the Spirit."

The fruit of the Spirit is love, joy, peace, patience, kindness, goodness, faithfulness, gentleness and self-control; against such things there is no law. — **Galatians 5:22 (ESV)**

The law could show people what was right and wrong, what sin was and what was not, but it could never make a person do good things out of love for God. Only the Spirit of God could. Living by the fruit of the Spirit was a whole new way of life.

Free to Fulfill the Law

When a person submits their life to Christ, the Spirit instills in them the desire to live for Him. This new motivation to love and serve Him propels people to naturally do the things that He wants. But the problem is sometimes Christians cut themselves off from the source of those things by believing the lie they don't need to know the Old Testament.

For example, sometimes people think if they go around and love people the best that we can, that's enough. The problem is everyone has a different view of love, don't they? What one person thinks exhibits love another might believe is quite cruel.

There needs to be a universal standard here, and that's what God provides through the law; the indwelling power of the Spirit provides the motivation and the strength.

The Old Testament law could never produce a heart that wanted to be obedient to God but praise God that is what every single follower of Jesus possesses now. New Testament believers have been given something that Old Testament saints didn't have: a desire to please God.

This was what the Galatians were responsible for as gentiles: to obey the law, by the leading of the Holy

Spirit who would take them one step beyond what was written.

A Holy Light

Isn't that what Jesus did when He talked about the law? Once when teaching on a beautiful hillside next to the Sea of Galilee, Jesus said:

> *You have heard that it was said to those of old, "You shall not murder; and whoever murders will be liable to judgment.' But I say to you that everyone who is angry with his brother will be liable to judgment.* — **Matthew 5:21–22 (ESV)**

"You have heard that it was said.... But I say..." Jesus taught His curious listeners. He had just proclaimed He did not come to abolish the law, but now turned the basic law upside down and interpreted it in its fullest, perfect sense—giving the heart motivation that needed to come behind the law.

This perfect instruction that leads to heart change is needed more at this time than ever before in a world that is casting God's law aside, throwing off morality and seeking total freedom outside of God. There's never been a time in history when it's been more important for the people of God to become that holy light.

Christians should look holier to the world than the nation of Israel did at its peak, because followers of Jesus know their Messiah personally and He has sent His

Spirit into each person to help them know Him even more.

The darker it gets, the brighter that light of Christ should shine.

Choosing to Obey

Kids who were raised by parents who loved them but established consequences for disobedience tend to rear their own kids the same way. I still remember hearing this from my own children once they had grown up. "Dad, we're grateful that you gave us consequences," they told me. Finally, they understood! They begin to respect the person who did that for them, so much so that they keep the rules whether there were consequences or not.

Similarly, Paul said now that the penalty of the law was gone, Christians were *free to keep the law*. How does that work? People tend to see the law as a have-to kind of thing, right?

When a believer appreciates the depths of what God has done for them—first in offering salvation, then showing them how to be holy, and ultimately in taking away the punishment for when they fail—their obedience should no longer be a "have to" requirement.

Instead, because of what Christ has done for us, they should be filled with "want to" desire to obey. Thus, real freedom is living by the Spirit, in Christ-like obedience to God!

WORKBOOK

Chapter 6 Questions

Question: Why do you need both the written Word and the Holy Spirit to live out your faith? How do you distinguish sin from righteousness?

_____

_____

_____

_____

_____

_____

_____

_____

_____

_____

_____

Question: When have you encountered agitators in the Body of Christ? What did they demand of you or others? What is the proper response to such agitators?

_____

_____

_____

_____

_____

_____

_____

_____

_____

_____

_____

Question: Are you a "have to" or "want to" believer? What is required to become a "want to" believer?

_____

_____

_____

_____

_____

_____

_____

_____

_____

_____

Action: Don't let fear, doubt, or agitators in the church lead you from the truth! Instead remain rooted in God's

Word and the leading of His Spirit in faith—not one or the other! Look to the Word and the Spirit to help you distinguish sin from the fruits of righteousness, because faith in Jesus doesn't get you off the hook for following God's commandments. To the contrary, show your love for Him by being the light of His righteousness in the world on a daily basis. Embrace your freedom to love God and your neighbor by being a "want to" believer, not a "have to"!

Chapter 6 Notes

_____

_____

_____

_____

_____

_____

_____

_____

_____

_____

_____

_____

_____

_____

_____

_____

_____

_____

_____

_____

_____

_____

_____

CHAPTER SEVEN

The Kingdom Versus Sameness

To the churches in Galatia: Grace and peace to you from God our Father and the Lord Jesus Christ, who gave Himself for our sins to rescue us from this present evil age, according to the will of our God and Father, to whom be glory forever and ever. Amen. — **Galatians 1:2–5 (ESV)**

And from those who seemed to be influential (what they were makes no difference to me; God shows no partiality)—those, I say, who seemed influential added nothing to me. On the contrary, when they saw that I've been entrusted with the gospel to the uncircumcised, just as Peter had been entrusted with the gospel to the circumcised... — **Galatians 2:6–7 (ESV)**

And when James, Cephas, and John, who seemed to be pillars, perceived the grace that was given to me, they gave the right hand of fellowship to Barnabas and me, that we should go to the Gentiles and they to the circumcised. — **Galatians 2:9 (ESV)**

President Ronald Reagan uttered perhaps the most famous words of his entire presidency in front of the Brandenburg Gate in Berlin in June of 1987. There President Reagan challenged Soviet Union General Secretary Mikhail Gorbachev to "tear down this wall." For fifty years, the Berlin Wall had been an icon of the conflict between the United States and the Soviet Union. The wall was finally torn down in 1989 and the citizens of East and West Berlin celebrated new unity. Breaking down barriers, however, is never simple. Even though the visual symbol of that hostility between the two nations had been removed, resentment and conflict would persist.

Paul's mission, too, was to help break down barriers—in his case, for Christ. He was dedicated to showing people that God had a plan to transition from this present evil age into the age to come—a plan to make a new creation out of all those who would become a part of it through faith in Jesus Christ.

Unfortunately, for the past two thousand years or so of history, this transition hasn't worked out very well. Jews and gentiles have been envious and jealous of each other, and those barriers have not broken down easily.

The church has not done much better. There are too many denominations to count! It's the same principle: envy and jealousy lead to barriers and divisions.

However, it is possible to learn how to live like Kingdom people—people of real faith for the age to come—instead of people who are wooed *to* this present, evil age. That's the ultimate importance of the book of Galatians.

Ritual over Religion?

What constitutes real faith? Often Christians function on ritual instead of what religion really is. Though some might think ritual was a problem only the Jews had. But the Christian church is built around ritual just as much—identifying ceremonies such as baptism and confirmation as acts that save.

Any religion over time tends to become institutionalized. I was in a church of about 1,500 people. I didn't realize how important rituals were—worship going on with a set routine, unchanging from year to year. One time I moved the offering from the middle of the service to the end.

I received cards and letters like you wouldn't believe. It was like I had just unleashed a flood. People truly believed God had ordained the service to run a certain way and that was why things always had to be in that order.

Religion over a period of time tends to become institutionalized, and sometimes this established order needs to be challenged or shaken up a bit to refocus and revitalize our spiritual lives and communities.

Isn't it easy to conclude, "If I can just get people to do this, then they're saved"? That's what the influencers in Galatia were doing: "If we can just get these new Christian gentiles to fully become Jews then they can be saved. They can't be saved before that because they're not in the covenant." These men wanted to make sure that the ritual was a part of them—because of the institution, not because of what it represented.

Then Paul came along and contradicted this belief; gentile believers already *were* in the Abrahamic covenant. Recall that Abraham believed God, obeyed God, and was declared righteous prior to any ritual. In the same way, the gentiles who believed in Jesus were declared righteous, too.

One Kingdom, Two Branches

However, gentile Christians came face to face with men from Jerusalem who were used to doing things a certain way. And when the men from Jerusalem found people who weren't following the rules, they stepped in to bring correction.

Christians do the same things today that those Jews were doing at that time. Without realizing it, some within the church have made it just a little bit more difficult for people, elevating themselves to a higher place.

Paul says that these false brothers wanted to make others slaves—slaves to the Jewish rituals that in Paul's estimation were not necessary. Peter also knew those rituals weren't necessary. It was not with perishable things such as silver or gold Jesus redeemed believers "from the futile ways inherited from your forefathers..." (1 Peter 1:18 ESV). Peter proclaimed, "but with the precious blood of Christ" (1 Peter 1:18–19). The King James Version says, "from your vain conversation received by tradition from your fathers" (1 Peter 1:18 KJV).

Rituals, sometimes labeled "tradition," could never save a person.

Now, consider the character Titus. Why was Titus invited on the trip? I see Titus as a test case. He was a fully-devoted gentile believer. Titus returned to Antioch after his time in Jerusalem uncircumcised—living proof that it was no longer necessary to convert and become a Jew.

Adding Nothing

In English, Galatians 2:6 almost sounds like Paul was passing off the rest of the brothers as if he disregarded those in authority and didn't care. Paul wrote, "And from those who seemed to be influential (what they were makes no difference to me; God shows no partiality)— those, I say, who seemed influential added nothing to me" (Galatians 2:6 ESV).

Yet Paul did make the effort to go up to meet them in Jerusalem, so he did care. He sought them to teach them the gospel; they simply didn't *add* anything to the gospel.

The people who were confronting Paul were accusing him of not receiving the whole gospel, not understanding the whole gospel, and not being in Jerusalem where the gospel was supposed to be centered. Ultimately, they were challenging his calling as an apostle. This is why Paul stresses so strongly his point that the Jerusalem leaders "added nothing."

The Right Hand of Fellowship

In Galatians 2:9 Paul used the phrase "the right hand of fellowship," which sheds additional light on division in the early church (Galatians 2:9 ESV). In Hebrew, this phrase meant something very specific in the Hebrew, which can be understood through the idea of ordination. In an ordination ceremony, an earthly body that has been given authority recognizes God's call on someone and agrees with it. Giving someone the right hand of fellowship meant they recognized God's call on that person's life and stood in full agreement with it.

Paul went to the apostles because he desired this agreement—an ordination of sorts. And naturally those who were against him could no longer say, "Paul, you're doing it the wrong way," because their very own body had said it was in full agreement with him.

What was that agreement? The other apostles would go to the Jews, or the circumcised, and Paul to the uncircumcised. The church had now established two different branches.

The Same, but Different

This division early in the life of the God's church has proved to be a major problem; the church has not recognized that there are still two branches. For 1,800 years the church has taught it has replaced the Jews— that because the Jews did not accept Jesus at His first coming, the church took the Jews' place. This false theology, known today as "replacement theology," finds its roots in this passage in passages such as Galatians 2:9.

But aren't all believers one in Christ? Paul said a few verses later in Galatians 3:28, "There is neither Jew nor Greek, there is neither slave nor free, there is no male and female, for you are all one in Christ Jesus" (Galatians 3:28 ESV).

It's important to differentiate between the concept of *oneness* and *sameness*. There's a difference between being one in agreement and being the same. Consider a marriage. A man and a woman come together, different in gender and role but unified—one—in Spirit. In the same way, while Jews and gentiles were one in equality and agreement, Paul taught they were still very different in role.

The disciples in Jerusalem recognized this and understood that God had called Paul out for a specific task: to go to the gentiles.

The church is one Body with many parts serving a different function. Nobody can say, "You're supposed to be exactly like me." No one can say to the foot, "You need to be a hand like me, because I'm better at grabbing things." The individuals within the church can be one, but can also still be the parts that they were made to be. Yes, God is a God of oneness but he's also a God of distinction, and from now on the Jews and the gentile Christians would follow separate paths.

Fitting In or Sticking Out

Paul had been working with the new church in Galatia, teaching believers they could come into the commonwealth of Israel as gentiles without being legally converted to Judaism.

After he left, Paul received a letter from the Galatians which basically said, "Well, we know what you said, Paul, but some people have come along and they've told us that we really need to be fully converted, so we're going ahead and doing that now."

That's not just a first-century problem; it's a problem modern-day believers must deal with. How do Christians look at others? Do they accept others unconditionally? Do followers of Jesus stand on truth, or on tradition?

Paul's reaction is harsh, his emotion spilling out onto the page.

> *You foolish Galatians! Who has bewitched you? Before your very eyes Jesus Christ was clearly portrayed as crucified. I would like to learn just one thing from you: Did you receive the Spirit by observing the law, or by believing what you heard? Are you so foolish? After beginning by means of the Spirit, are you now trying to finish by means of the flesh?* — **Galatians 3:1–3 (NIV)**

Paul was quite upset—not surprisingly. The word 'bewitched' in Greek means "to be controlled by someone else or to be acting in an unusual manner." The Galatians, in Paul's eyes, were confused and acting irrationally.

Who Has Bewitched You?

Who was controlling the Galatians? Who were the influencers in this situation?

As we discussed earlier, a group of gentiles had fully converted to Judaism, going through the process of circumcision and baptism and all the rites. Paul came along and said, "Guess what? You can be saved without that. You gentiles are okay just the way you are."

People don't like it when they have jumped through hoops only to have somebody come along and tell them none of that matters. That is the issue Paul was addressing in Galatians 3:1. Those who had converted to Judaism earlier were busy persuading others they needed to convert too in order to be truly or fully saved.

But Paul asked, "Are you so foolish? After beginning by means of the Spirit, are you now trying to finish by means of the flesh?" (Galatians 3:3 NIV). That term "finish" is very important. What was their goal?

The Proof of the Holy Spirit

These people believed they needed to convert to Judaism to be part of the "group." They loved God and wanted to do what was right, so they were willing to do what needed to be done to ensure their salvation—this was their goal.

But Paul was passionate about making sure they understood they did not need to do anything more to be saved. They had received the Holy Spirit without adding any external requirements to their faith. Paul, Peter, and even people within the church in Galatia had seen that the Holy Spirit had visibly come upon these people, even though they were gentiles.

In today's world Christians don't see the activity of the Holy Spirit quite as visibly. But here Paul's evidence for salvation was the activity of the Spirit. His firm reminder was that the process of salvation began when they received the Holy Spirit—it had nothing to do with keeping the law.

Often, this passage is interpreted to mean the Holy Spirit has superseded the law, but that's not what it's about.

The Shovel and the Spoon

Imagine if I gave someone two tools to complete a certain task, a shovel and a spoon. Which tools the person chose to use would on depend on the task in hand, correct?

Suppose I asked that person to dig a big hole in the backyard. If I came back and found them digging the hole with a spoon, I would question this person's sanity! Now suppose I said, "Go into the house—I've made you some soup." If I saw the shovel in the soup I would have that same reaction!

Which of the two tools is bad—the shovel or the spoon? Neither one is bad, of course. The best tool depends on the job it is needed for. So it is with the Spirit and God's *torah*. Both are valid, but they play different roles. Paul was teaching about salvation through the Spirit as well as holiness and the law.

Holiness grows believers to become useful to God, and what holiness looks like is revealed through His Word. Therefore, God's *torah* is absolutely necessary for what it was intended to do, and that is to bring people into a holy relationship with God.

Remember, though Paul was preaching against circumcision and other Jewish rituals for gentile believers, he never said God's *torah* was bad or had been annulled. When he went to prison at the end of his life he was able to proclaim, "I have never ceased to do what the Torah has commanded me." But he knew very clearly that the law never saved him.

This is the same distinction believers today need to draw, instead of saying God's *torah*, (His instruction) is not needed anymore. Rejecting God's instruction leads the church down the wrong path, making it useless.

A Peculiar People

What is it about the church that makes us useful to the world? The relative usefulness of the church goes back to the idea of holiness. I would hope most believers would want to be holy. But what if I said, "How many of you want to be *peculiar* in this world?" Likely not many would raise a hand! Yet that's what holiness means: it means *set apart*. Paul said elsewhere that followers of Jesus were a "peculiar people..." (Titus 2:14 KJV). That means believers would be called to stand out, to not blend in.

I know that in high school, for example, a teen's priority is the opposite. They do not want to stick out but rather to blend in. That doesn't change a great deal until they mature enough not to care much what people think. For some that might never happen!

This attitude will make a Christian useless to God. God wants His children set apart. In fact, He wants believers to be different from the rest of the world. Jesus said, "You are the salt of the earth. But if the salt loses its saltiness, how can it be made salty again? It is no longer good for anything, except to be thrown out and trampled underfoot" (Matthew 5:13 NIV).

Holiness is what God's *torah* is for—to make people holy so that they affect the world instead of allowing the world to affect them.

The Pain of Being Different

Paul continued by saying, "Have you suffered so much in vain—if it really was in vain?" (Galatians 3:4 NIV). How have they suffered? Whenever people are in a group they typically want to be like the rest in the group—to be accepted. And I think that was probably the case in Galatia.

These God-fearing gentiles were a part of the synagogue. They loved God and they loved the people they were with. But they felt like they were still different. They weren't a part of the group. And so they went through this process to get rid of that distinction and become fully Jewish.

Did that end their problem? No, because they were living in a Roman culture. Now it was the gentiles and the Romans who had a problem with them because they no longer worshiped Caesar or Roman gods. Not only were they different from the Jewish believers, but they were also outcasts in the Roman world, separate from their own families and friends.

Paul saw what had happened, and he knew they had gone through their transformation for nothing—even though it was an attempt to please God and be sure of salvation. Paul wrote, "Does he who supplies the Spirit to you and works miracles among you do so by works of the law, or by hearing with faith…" (Galatians 3:5 ESV).

There is nothing anyone can ever do to earn salvation, except believe in the Lord Jesus Christ.

Yet Jesus told His followers, "You are the light of the world" (Matthew 5:14 ESV). Believers are to light up the doorway for others to enter by through obeying the instructions in His Word.

Therefore, Paul called believers to be holy—peculiar and different from the rest of the world. And that's a heavy calling because just like the gentile believers in Galatia, believers today would rather fit in than stand out. It's not something any human being naturally wants to do, as we will explore further in the next chapter—yet it is what our faith and our love for God requires of us.

WORKBOOK

Chapter 7 Questions

Question: When have you encountered a problematic ritual or tradition among believers? How did you know it was problematic? What was, or is, the proper response to such institutional pressures, exactly—and how do you know?

_____

_____

_____

_____

_____

_____

_____

_____

_____

_____

_____

_____

Question: What is "oneness" in the context of God's Kingdom? What does it require, and why is it desirable? How can you pursue oneness in the Body, individually and collectively?

_____

_____

_____

_____

_____

_____

_____

_____

_____

_____

_____

Question: What is "sameness" in the context of the Body of Christ? Provide a few examples. Why is it an obstacle to the Kingdom?

_____

_____

_____

_____

_____

_____

_____

_____

_____

_____

Action: Beware of ritual that tries to lead the Body of Christ away from real faith and real religion! When tradition stands against truth, stand up and stick your neck out for truth—even when it's not the easy or comfortable thing to do. Don't let anyone convince you that oneness in faith and love requires God's children to demonstrate sameness in all things. Likewise, resist the urge to pressure others in the church to be the same as you; instead, recognize the natural differences God has created among His people. In fact, don't be afraid to stand out from the crowd. To the contrary, be holy—different and set apart for God's purpose. Choose God's Kingdom over church culture every time!

Chapter 7 Notes

CHAPTER EIGHT

Culture Clash

But now that you have come to know God, or rather to be known by God, how can you turn back again to the weak and worthless elementary principles of the world, whose slaves you want to be once more? You observe days and months and seasons and years! I am afraid I may have labored over you in vain. Brothers, I entreat you, become as I am, for I also have become as you are. You did me no wrong. — ***Galatians 4:9–12 (ESV)***

Occasionally I am asked: "Why don't New Testament believers keep the Old Testament festivals of God, or God's day of rest, the Sabbath?" Whenever I confront this question with someone, Galatians 4:9–12 is the passage to which they turn.

Many interpret these verses to mean Paul was chastising those who were keeping the New Moon celebrations, the festivals, and the Sabbath—that Paul told them they didn't need to do keep those special days and shouldn't be keeping those festivals.

But is that what Galatians 4:9–12 really means? Remember to whom Paul was talking—not the Jews but the gentile believers in Galatia. And their culture was completely different from Jewish culture.

Waiting for Our Inheritance

Because the groups were so different, Paul used the idea of a Roman family to help these gentile believers connect and understand Jewish culture. Back in Galatians 4:1–2 Paul had said, "I mean that the heir, as long as he is a child, is no different from a slave, though he is the owner of everything, but he is under guardians and managers until the date set by his father" (ESV).

A typical family household consisted of both children and slaves who lived in the house together. What happened if the father died and the oldest son was not yet of age? Did the son take control of the household at that point? No. He would still be under a household manager until he reached the age where he could take control of those things. But that didn't make him any less an heir.

Paul used this concept to illustrate how the gentiles had been under managers up to that point because they hadn't reached that age where they could take control of the blessing. Recall the blessing did not come from being a Jew but from being in Abraham through faith in the Messiah. According to Paul, gentiles weren't part of this blessing at first because the time had not yet come.

He continued in Galatians 4:3, "In the same way we also, when we were children..." (ESV). Paul wrote the gentiles were also under managers for a time, until they became heirs through believing Jews. Gentiles and Jews were the same in that respect. Both had come into their inheritance.

The Elemental Principles

At this point in his letter to the Galatians, Paul dove into a difficult topic:

> *In the same way we also, when we were children, were enslaved to the elemental principles of the world.* — **Galatians 4:3 (ESV)**

This scripture is sometimes very hard to understand. It's ambiguous in both the Greek and in the Hebrew. What did it mean to be enslaved to the elemental principles of the world?

There are really two options. One is that these "elemental principles" refer to both God's *torah* and Judaism. The other possibility is that they referred to paganism and idolatry.

As I mentioned, most people interpret Paul's teaching here to mean, "Why in the world are you going back and celebrating the Jewish festivals?" The "days and months and seasons and years" (Galatians 4:10 NIV) refer to weekly, monthly, seasonal, and yearly feasts—*moedim* in Hebrew, God's set or appointed times.[10] It appears Paul was upset because they were celebrating those things.

But Paul was not talking about the godly holidays, the festivals that God set up Himself. God didn't say, "These are the holidays that *you Jews* need to celebrate." In Leviticus 23:2 God said, "These are the appointed feasts of the LORD that you shall proclaim as holy convocations; *they are my appointed feasts*" (ESV, emphasis added). The feasts were God's holy appointed times that he gave to Israel. Why would Paul ever want to stop what God initiated?

Remember to whom Paul was talking: the people in Galatia. They were gentile believers who had not converted to Judaism. These gentiles were coming out of a culture of paganism and idolatry.

Doesn't it make more sense that Paul was talking about putting a stop to paganism and adultery, not to Judaism and the law of Moses—which Paul himself kept and had praised through his entire letter to the Galatians up to this point?

Pagan Worship by Law

Every person in the Roman Empire who was not part of an approved religion like Judaism—in other words, all gentiles, including God-fearing followers of Christ—was required to worship Caesar and all the gods of the Roman pantheon through weekly, monthly and yearly pagan festivals.

Imagine being a gentile believer in that situation, obligated under the government to worship idols. These Christians were stuck between a desire to worship the one true God, on the one hand, and their culture, families, and authorities, on the other. They were subject to punishment, imprisonment, or worse if they didn't observe these things.

But here is what would eliminate all of that: you could be fully converted and become a Jew. That would take all the pressure off you, because Jews were exempt.

Paul was not writing to Jews about their festivals, but to these gentile believers who were up against a whole set of other issues—how to live in a culture that was hostile to what they believed and forced them to keep pagan festivals.

Paul was aware the gentile believers were caving to surrounding pressure. Frustrated, Paul wondered if he had wasted his time with them (Galatians 4:11).

United in Purpose

In Galatians, Paul attempted to bring together two groups of people who historically had a very hard time getting along. He focused commonalities. Both were like children who are under a master until they become heirs; according to Paul, until either Jew or gentiles accepted Jesus, they were both children of God who had not yet come of age.

Modern-day believers are like that, too. What makes people one is not that they are Jews and Christians, but that they believe in Jesus.

Paul affirmed this saying, "Because you are sons, God has sent the Spirit of His Son into our hearts, crying, '*Abba*! Father!'" (Galatians 4:6 ESV). The disciples had seen gentiles receive the Holy Spirit of God the same way the Jews had and recognized that was what makes the two groups one. In Christ there are no Jews or Greeks, slaves or free people, males or females; all are one in purpose.

Become As I Am

Try to imagine a scenario in which Paul would say, "Don't keep the law of God. Stop doing holidays; holidays are no good. We shouldn't be doing that even if God did set them up himself." And yet the majority of the church reads Galatians 4:9–10 and says, "See, it's a good thing the Old Testament is done away with because we're not supposed to be celebrating all of those old holidays anyway."

Galatians 4:9–12 is about paganism and idolatry, not the Jewish festivals. Knowing Paul and the rest of the book of Galatians, there is no other conclusion.

Paul, a *torah*-observant Jew, never stopped participating in the festivals. He wrote next, "Brothers, I entreat you, become as I am" (Galatians 4:12 ESV). Paul had come to the end of his life and said he still was able to declare he had never ceased to keep every single part of the law.

Galatians 4:9–12 is a lesson on observing the law and praying to God—*Abba,* Father. The Spirit was the center of Paul's life. So he told the Galatians to become as he was, in that he loved God and prayed to Him in a personal way and had the Spirit within him.

But don't miss the end of Galatians 4:12 where Paul affirmed: "...for I became like you" (NIV). How had he become like the Galatians? Had he given up keeping the *torah*? No, "I have become like you" means Paul kept the law because he loved God, but he also knew he did not have to put his faith in the law to make him righteous. He gave all of that up for the sheer knowledge of relying on the righteousness of the Messiah.

This phrase "I have become like you" has sometimes been misunderstood to imply a chameleon-like adaptability. In fact, it sheds a light on Paul's approach to building relationships and making disciples. We'll be looking at this in the next chapter.

Paul's one "rule" for the church was that they remain as they were. If circumcised when called by God, then a believer should stay a Jew. If not circumcised when called, the believer should stay a gentile. The only things that made a difference were faith and the belief that the Spirit indwelt believers, making them one.

Don't Conform to the Culture

Once gentiles came to know Jesus, they were one with Jews in Spirit and had the same Father—and Paul said they could no longer go back to pagan worship. He warned them not to let culture push them into its own mold.

Believers today will experience every kind of persecution, every kind of effort to conform to the world. Paul warns harshly against this, so exasperated he said, "Have I wasted my time with you? Have I not taught you anything in the process? This is basic. Why in the world would you go back to worshipping an idol, a false god?"

Followers of Jesus must rely only on what God thinks, not what man thinks.

Jesus and Paul were *torah* observers. They loved and kept the Word of God. They celebrated the God-initiated holidays and festivals as unto Him. Paul never insinuated that worshipping God in this way should stop.

Do believers today need to keep the festivals? Recall that Jesus didn't "abolish the Law or the Prophets"—what Christians now recognize as books of the Old Testament—"but to fulfill them" (Matthew 5:17 ESV). Rather, Jesus is the fullness of interpretation on the law of Moses. He is the "substance to come" spoken of by Paul in Colossians. Christ is the fulfillment of the Jewish festivals.

Truth in Love

The surrounding culture tells people what they *want* to hear, not what they *need* to hear. That's why it is so important to rely on Jesus, who came full of truth and love. Love without truth tells people what they want to hear.

Jesus was the embodiment of both love and truth. And that's why he was that perfect representative of God, because He spoke the truth in love.

The truth is, in the course of our lives we all encountered "sandpaper" people, or people who are hard to be around because they are different. But the people of God are called to be holy, and part of that holiness means believers are to love one another—which includes supporting and encouraging people who are different.

That one concept will change any marriage. Husbands and wives will have a rough and rocky road if their desire is to make the other person in the relationship the same as they. Every marriage involves two people—and often, differences attract. Learning to start encouraging those differences instead of trying to squelch them will help prevent a bumpy marriage.

This concept is true about the family of God.

The moment a person accepts Jesus, they become part of the family of God. But that journey as a believer will be rough if the person's desire is to make everyone exactly like them. Believers can be one, but they don't have to be the *same*.

God's desire has always been the same for His people, circumcised and uncircumcised alike: to be holy; to be different; to be as the Bible says they are supposed to be—a peculiar people.

The book of Galatians is all about belonging. The gentiles' desire was to belong in a Jewish world, and similarly, believers today need to understand how they fit into culture today. But Galatians also looks at the broader underlying theme of how God's people relate to the wider society.

Above all, Paul's letter to the Galatians is about how followers of Jesus belong together as part of God's new creation. Understanding this determines the direction a believer will take as part of the people of God. Will they pull together? Or will they become different and stand against what's going on in the world? Or will they blend in so they are indistinguishable from everyone else?

Every follower of Jesus will need to make this choice.

.

WORKBOOK

Chapter 8 Questions

Question: What kinds of things does the surrounding culture pressure you to do? How do you know where to draw the line?

_____

_____

_____

_____

_____

_____

_____

_____

_____

_____

_____

Question: How, exactly, do you know you're following Jesus and not the ways of the world in the course of your daily life?

_____
_____
_____
_____
_____
_____
_____
_____
_____
_____
_____
_____

Question: How does the world know you belong to Christ? How can you better show them, exactly?

_____
_____
_____
_____
_____
_____
_____
_____
_____
_____
_____

Action: Just as you stand for God's truth over false teaching, faithless ritual, and the tendency to sameness within the Body of Christ, stand fast for truth when faced with pressure to conform to the unbelieving world as well. Follow Jesus, His Word, and His Holy Spirit, and let the world see the difference they make in your life!

Chapter 8 Notes

CHAPTER NINE

One Kingdom for All, All for One

Being much concerned about the rise of denominations in the church, John Wesley [told] of a dream he had. In the dream, he was ushered to the gates of Hell. There he asked, "Are there any Presbyterians here?" "Yes!" came the answer. Then he asked, "Are there any Baptists? Any Episcopalians? Any Methodist?" The answer was Yes! each time. Much distressed, Wesley was then ushered to the gates of Heaven. There he asked the same question, and the answer was No! "No?" To this, Wesley asked, "Who then is inside?" The answer came back, "There are only Christians here."[11]

God accepts everyone, regardless of social, religious, or ethnic background. The first disciples needed to wrestle with concept, a vastly different concept for that day. Paul was probably nervous about telling the top religious leaders about his work with the gentiles. Maybe that's why he spoke to these authority figures in private.

A New Kind of Kingdom

But God had been working throughout the church and especially in Peter, who had had a similar revelation about gentile believers and was coming to the same conclusion. This is why they gathered in Jerusalem to work out some of the issues that had bubbled up.

In fact, Peter said, "I now realize how true it is that God does not show favoritism but accepts from every nation the one who fears him and does what is right" (Acts 10:34–35 NIV).

Isn't that an amazing conclusion for Peter to reach in that day and age? It's easier to believe God accepts everyone now, almost two thousand years later, but that was counterculture in the first century. Before Jesus' death and resurrection, a person couldn't come into the Kingdom of God until they became a Jew.

How did Peter come to realize that God accepted everyone? He had seen some amazing things that astounded him. He saw the Holy Spirit come upon a gentile named Cornelius based on his belief and faith in Jesus Christ alone, not because of his nationality or background. That was a mind-boggling thing for Peter. Because of this, Peter was assured salvation was not based on any kind of nationality but was available to any person if they believed God and wanted to do what was right. That's what God was looking for.

This was a massive challenge for the early church. It's also a massive challenge for believers today! People may tell themselves they welcome everyone just as they are in the name of Jesus, but is this really what people believe?

It's time to face up to the truth and admit that in the twenty-first century people may still set limitations and boundaries on what God can achieve in church.

Breaking Fences

Jesus was constantly accused of breaking the law. But what He really broke was the fence *around* the law.

The Jews used to build a metaphorical fence around the law to protect it. For example, the law said, "You shall not take the name of the Lord your God in vain…" (Exodus 20:7 ESV). The Jews believed the only way to keep this commandment was to never say the Lord's name at all. Thus, every time they happened upon the Lord's name when reading the Torah, they would say *HaShem,* meaning "the Name." This, they believed, guarded them from any possibility of falling into sin.

Was it unlawful to say the name of God? No. But they built a fence around God's instruction so they would never mistakenly infringe upon the law.

The law said a follower of God must not be defiled by idols, so the Jews built another fence. They said, "Okay, we're not even going to eat with people who *might be* defiled by idols, so we won't eat with the gentiles." Over centuries, this mindset evolved within the community of Jews, who eventually believed eating with gentiles was a sin.

A Difficult Lesson

In Acts 10 Peter was called to go to a gentile's house. Obviously, since Peter was a Jew, this was a problem: there were many strict laws of separation, and prevailing Jewish opinion held that sharing a meal with a gentile could defile a person.

Peter pointed this out when he went to see Cornelius. "You yourselves know how unlawful it is for a Jew to associate with or visit anyone of another nation," (Acts 10:28 ESV) Peter said. However, God had shown Peter in a vision that no person should be called "common" or "unclean." Peter understood God was doing something new, and that God "shows no partiality" (Acts 10:34 ESV).

Peter had said, "Now I know that no man is unclean." Notice Peter didn't say no *food* was unclean, although his vision was about food. Rather, he realized it was okay to eat with gentiles because what God makes pure is pure (Acts 10:28).

Unfortunately, when Peter traveled down from Jerusalem to see how things were going in Antioch—to the church where Paul and Barnabas were preaching—he suddenly forgot that lesson.

Fellowship at Antioch

In this amazing church Jews and gentiles were meeting together, fellowshipping together, and eating together as brothers and sisters—not as first-class and second-class citizens, but as equals.

How excited they must have been that the apostles were coming from Jerusalem and they could ask Peter about the Master—the one that they had only heard about! Now they could hear firsthand information about what it was like to be a disciple of Jesus.

Yet any time something good is going on in the church the enemy—the adversary—will be close behind ready to stir things up. And that's exactly what happened.

In addition to Peter's group, another group whom Paul called "the circumcision party" (Galatians 2:12 HCSB) had arrived in Galatia to spy on the infant church. These spies were the same people who had said gentile believers needed to be circumcised and become full Jews to be part of the Kingdom.

Not surprisingly, this group also believed Jewish believers shouldn't eat with gentiles.

Peer Pressure on Peter

Just as young people often have to wade through years of peer pressure in middle and high school, so did the early church. Peter was eating with gentiles when people began grumble. Perhaps Peter thought, "Oh well, maybe I should watch it. Maybe I should eat at my own table and try not to cause a ruckus." Peter succumbed to first-century peer pressure.

Picture the scene: gentile believers were enjoying a meal with Jewish believers, when all of a sudden one Jewish man pulled away and refused to eat or fellowship with them. And it didn't go unnoticed.

Paul knew he had to confront the issue. The very thing he'd been trying to build up— fellowship between Jews and gentiles—was being threatened. He knew the result could lead to a sharp division within the church, so he had to act. In his letter Peter said, "I opposed him to his face, because he stood condemned" (Galatians 2:11 ESV). Peter was condemned by his own words, because he had earlier accepted that God shows no partiality and no one is unclean in Christ.

Et Tu, Barnabas?

Paul was very outspoken in what he believed. He told Peter right to his face that he stood condemned. Before those dissension-loving men showed up, Peter had eaten freely with the gentiles, but as soon as the men from the circumcision party arrived, he drew back out of fear. And the rest of the Jews acted hypocritically along with him.

Surprisingly, Barnabas was led astray by the hypocrisy. He was the one who began the church in Antioch that first saw the Jews and the gentiles coming together! Barnabas means "son of encouragement," and that's really who he was—a great encouragement to Paul.

How then was he led astray? No doubt Barnabas was trying to encourage others, but he let his encouragement lapse into sympathy or tolerance for a point of view against which he should have taken a stand. This can all too easily happen to believers today as well.

Factions in the Church

All churches have issues. Even the first-century church made up of men who had walked and talked with Jesus had issues.

Differences, however, should never cause factions in the church. This division wasn't really about the law, because God's Word never forbid the Jews to eat with other nations. It wasn't even about food, because Jews and gentiles were eating the same food. They were worshiping together. They were hearing the same Word of God.

It was about those man-instituted fences constructed around God's instruction, and it resulted in believers pulling back and withdrawing from each other. This seed of hypocrisy was causing people within the early church to divide.

Time for Some Soul-Searching

Unfortunately, this issue didn't end in the first century. Believers have always had differences, whether culturally, politically, or even theologically. But withdrawing from the Body goes against God's Word. Human beings have an innate desire to associate with people who are similar, and this unfortunately this happens within the church, too. Factions form over time, and before long, sharp divisions form.

Acts 15 introduces what was called "the Jerusalem Council." This was a gathering of believers who met to decide all over again what they had already determined at the time of Paul's visit. I'm sure the criticism wasn't easy for Peter to deal with, but he must have taken this to heart because by the time the Jerusalem Council convened, believers agreed what Paul was endorsing was right.

All churches have issues, but they can be handled correctly with the help of God. He has placed the Body of Christ together in the church with people of different beliefs and different spiritual gifts so that it will be the people He wants. It is critical that individuals within the Body resist the temptation to pull others over to their "team," and instead learn to love those who have different beliefs or opinions.

United We Stand

Remember the Three Musketeers, and their motto, "All for one and one for all"? Although these three men were each very different, their motto was about unity.

That's exactly where Paul began this section in Galatians 3:26. He wanted to show Jews and gentiles that despite their differences, they were on the same side, so he said, "You are all sons of God, through faith" (Galatians 3:26 ESV)—in other words, through belief and obedience to Jesus Christ. Often believers today believe this verse was written to them.

But Paul was writing to those two very different groups who were highly suspicious of each other. The Jews were trying to say, "You gentiles, the only way you can come and be part of the sons of God is if you go through the Mosaic law and are fully converted to being a Jew. Then we'll let you into the club."

The gentile Christians were just beginning to learn about God and were suspicious of the Jews. Perhaps they thought, "Why are these mean Jewish people putting all these strict regulations on us? This was supposed to be something of joy and love and being a part of the family of God."

And the battle has been a part of history ever since. One side has always mistrusted the other.

The Bookshop

What are relationships like between Jews and Christians today? It's kind of a mixed bag, isn't it? There's still a lot of doubt and mistrust.

When I was in Israel, we stopped at this little bookshop that sold both Jewish and Christian items. I was with a group of about twenty, and we crowded into the bookstore. And man working behind the counter saw us, shut the door and put the "closed" sign up.

Now that scared me a little bit. I thought, "Uh-oh, I'm trapped in here now!"

But the man told us he was a Messianic Jew. As he relayed many stories about well-meaning Christians who came into the shop and tried to convert him, we sat around the store laughing. He said, "You know, some of these things that Christians say to us are a little bit off-putting. They act like we have no idea who God is when we've been reading His Word for thousands of years."

There exists today a kind of tension between Jews and gentiles. But Paul experienced it at its peak, at the church's inception. Paul was one man working tirelessly to try to get these two groups to work together.

Embracing Differences

*There is neither Jew nor Greek, there is neither slave nor free, there is no male or female, for you are all one in Christ Jesus. — **Galatians 3:28 (ESV)***

In Galatians 3:28, Paul did not mean there was now one kind of new person—no more Jews and no more gentiles, but everyone the same. In fact, what Paul taught was exactly the opposite. Both were supposed to exist side by side, working together—one in purpose. Like the Musketeers, who were three different men with a common mission to protect the king and to protect France, believers can embrace differences but still be united.

Though united in Christ, however, they are nowhere near the same—as a matter of fact, in many case individuals within the Body of Christ are exact opposites! And unfortunately, the church has done its best to eliminate those differences, not embrace them.

The Family of God

Only let each person lead the life that the Lord has assigned to him, and to which God has called him. This is my rule in all the churches. Was anyone at the time of his call already circumcised? Let him not seek to remove the marks of circumcision. Was anyone at the time of his call uncircumcised? Let him not seek circumcision. For neither circumcision counts for anything nor uncircumcision, but keeping the commandments of God. — **1 Corinthians 7:17–19 (ESV)**

By contrast, regardless of whether a believer was Jewish or a gentile, Paul exhorted believers that all could be a part of the family of God. No one needed to change. The believers were one, but they didn't have to worry about being the same in every area of life. They just needed to be unified in love for God and others.

Love One Another

The apostle John wrote about Jesus' command to love others: "A new command I give you: Love one another. As I have loved you, so you must love one another" (John 13:34 NIV).

The root of the New Testament word for the phrase 'one another' is actually about differences.[12] Loving one another does not mean loving people who are similar. In fact, it means to love those who are different. That is the true mark of a follower of Christ.

Jesus taught this concept throughout His ministry on earth. John continued, "By this everyone will know that you are my disciples, if you love one another" (John 13:35 NIV).

There is no great spiritual benefit to loving people who are friends, or who are the same. But people will take notice when believers love people who are vastly different; it will be a witness to the world of Christ's love.

One in Purpose

Thus, Galatians 3:28 does not teach believers they need to be the same. Later in the verse Paul said, "There is no male and female" (Galatians 3:28 ESV). Males and females are physically not the same, and yet they can be one in purpose, in a marriage.

It was the same thing with slaves and free men. In his letter to Philemon, Paul sent Onesimus back to his slave-owner, telling him he was one with Onesimus because they were both believers. In other words, the desire for both even as master and slave should be to please the Father. And that meant both had to respect each other.

The differences were not eliminated; Onesimus didn't stop being a slave. But their differences no longer mattered because their purpose was now the same.

Jesus said in John 17, "I only came to do what the Father has asked me to do. And I did everything exactly the way He wanted me to; we were exactly one in purpose." (John 15:19). Jesus prayed for every man, woman, and child who would believe in Him, knowing each would possess various personalities and gifts. He prayed that none of that would matter because their purpose was now exactly the same as His.

Christians are called to be one in Christ because they each have the same purpose. If baptized, if a person has surrendered their life to Jesus as Lord and Savior, the follower of Jesus now should do what Jesus said to do.

God is one, but what is amazing is that the Body of Christ was put together with many individuals with special gifts and abilities. No two of people are exactly alike. That's a good thing!

When the church begins to see those differences as the way God has made His children, it changes everything. Believers will remain one *in purpose*. They can be different from one another, yet encourage each other's differences. If this isn't what you are observing and experiencing within the church, then it's time to start changing the church culture in line with God's Word.

Chapter 9 Questions

Question: What kinds of barriers or fences do people try to erect around the law and God's Word?

_____

_____

_____

_____

_____

_____

_____

_____

_____

_____

_____

Question: Where do you encounter factions in the Body of Christ? How can you respond to such factiousness in a Christ-like way?

_____

_____

_____

_____

_____

_____

_____

_____

_____

_____

_____

Question: What are some specific ways you can help further unity in the Body of Christ?

_____

_____

_____

_____

_____

_____

_____

_____

_____

_____

Action: Like Jesus, break down barriers that try to separate people from the moral law of Scripture, rather than trying to break or discard the law and God's instructions. You might not do everything the same way as every other believer, but the scriptural commandments and teachings of God are for you and all believers. Though we shouldn't try or want to be identical in every respect, unity of faith, love, and purpose with your fellow members of the Body of Christ is the goal. Embrace each other's differences and the diverse ways you serve the Lord. Avoid factiousness and be one in Christ—united for God as His loving family!

Chapter 9 Notes

_____

_____

_____

_____

_____

_____

_____

_____

_____

_____

_____

_____

_____

_____

_____

_____

_____

_____

_____

_____

_____

_____

_____

CHAPTER TEN

The Ministry of Reconciliation

Brothers, if anyone is caught in any transgression, you who are spiritual should restore him in a spirit of gentleness. Keep watch on yourself, les you too be tempted. — **Galatians 6:1 (ESV)**

Dietrich Bonhoeffer was a German Lutheran pastor, theologian, and author who loved Jesus and rebuked comfortable Christianity. In addition, he was an anti-Nazi rebel who ended up imprisoned for His work against Hitler. Bonhoeffer forgave his Nazi guards, and even shared his meager meals with them,[13] but stopped short of reconciling with them.

It's possible to forgive people who hurt, without reconciling. However, God calls believers to step out to a place where they are often uncomfortable, and to trust God with bringing people together who outside of Christ could never even speak.

Paul had been dealing with two groups of people and told them the truth. He had made it absolutely clear that they were not required to become a Jew in order to be saved. He rebuked certain people, making them unhappy.

Paul, like all truthful people, ruffled feathers. Jesus was the same, "full of grace and truth" (John 1:14 ESV). Paul now turned his attention to reconciliation, a ministry Jesus pronounced to His disciples.

People are much better at fighting than at reconciling. Reconciliation is hard because of pride. When a person is offended, human tendency is to fight for what is owed and can now be rightfully collect. They might place blame on another, or try and gather others to be on their side—all acts that actually hurt reconciliation.

How was it possible for Paul to bring two people groups back together who had a longstanding hatred of each other? Should he have done what has become common in the West—start a new church or form a new denomination?

The Two Conditions

Paul didn't want to see that happen; he wanted to see reconciliation and healing, for this was God's heart. Two things were absolutely necessary for godly restoration, and Paul addressed them in Galatians 6:1: "Brothers, if anyone is caught in any transgression, you who are spiritual should restore him in a spirit of gentleness. Keep watch on yourself, lest you too be tempted" (ESV).

First, Galatians 6:1 identifies who Paul gives permission to proceed with reconciliation: "you who are spiritual" (ESV). Paul had just talked about what it means to be spiritual, in chapter 5: "If we live by the Spirit, let us also keep in step with the Spirit" (Galatians 5:25 ESV). and be obedient and humble, daily seeking out truth in God's Word. The first step in restoration is therefore character-related—to assume a correct posture before God and others.

Those who are not spiritual choose not to obey God. Those who make this choice have no right then reconciling people within the church. They will likely judge others by their own personal standard, not God's. Jesus said instead believers must pull the log out of their own eye before confronting someone else with their sin. Paul said the same thing.

Second, Galatians 6:1 says restoration must be done with gentleness, and one's motivation must stem from deep love and concern for the other person.

Confronting people because of a difference in opinion, a dislike or with the attitude of "Aha! Gotcha!" indicates an ungodly character issue, and reconciliation will not work. Paul said Christians must watch themselves closely and examine their heartfelt reasons for desiring reconciliation.

Healing Relationships

Love and concern for the other person must come first, but typically human are most concerned for their own needs. Believers can never be ministers of reconciliation with that attitude.

Jesus cared about reconciliation, didn't He? Think again of the woman who was caught in adultery. The

Pharisees sought to judge her for her sin, bringing her before Jesus:

> *Jesus returned to the Mount of Olives, but early the next morning he was back again at the Temple. A crowd soon gathered, and he sat down and taught them. As he was speaking, the teachers of religious law and the Pharisees brought a woman who had been caught in the act of adultery. They put her in front of the crowd. "Teacher," they said to Jesus, "this woman was caught in the act of adultery. The law of Moses says to stone her. What do you say?"* – **John 8:1–5 (NLT)**

Jesus could have said, "Yep, you sinned. Take her away, stone her." But He cared more about reconciliation. He didn't say, "You're guilty," or "You're innocent." He said, "Go, and sin no more" (John 8:11 KJV).

The teachers of the law were more concerned about the fences erected around God's instruction than about the woman, who was broken. The woman needed restoration with God, but instead these leaders condemned her for her actions. Jesus, however, saw her heart and who she was in her Father's eyes: a child of the Most High God.

This is what reconciliation is about; it's not about right and wrong, but about relationships coming back together. Ultimately, reconciliation is about people being restored in their relationship with God.

A Different Way

Let us not become weary in doing good, for at the proper time we will reap a harvest if we do not give up. Therefore, as we have opportunity, let us do good to all people, especially to those who belong to the family of believers. — **Galatians 6:9–10 (NIV)**

Followers of Christ are family and have been called to put each other first. That's the only way reconciliation will happen because, let's face it: the last thing people who have been hurt want to do is to make themselves vulnerable again. If owed money, the last thing people naturally want to do is forgive that debt. The bigger the debt, the harder it is to forgive.

Paul made it very clear that what he expected from the Galatians next was reconciliation—for them to come together in unity to bear one another's burdens and for each one to carry the load that God has given them.

And let's face it: this is a hard task for the church. It's a hard task for individuals, too, especially when society communicates people should do whatever they personally think is right regardless of what God's Word says.

Believers must take the first step and go against what society says; instead, they must trust God for what He says is best. They must strive to keep the Body unified and make God's priority their priority.

All Things to All People

The church tends to repeat certain phrases, and often people don't know where those verses can be found in Scripture. One of the favorites is, "Judge not, that you be not judged" (Matthew 7:1 ESV). That's how people silence others when they don't want to hear what they're saying.

However, using a verse like this manipulates people and is often a result of taking the Scripture out of context.

The Chameleon

Previously Paul had said to the Galatians; "Become like me, for I became like you" (Galatians 4:12 NIV). Recall that Paul kept the law because of his love for God but, like the gentiles, he didn't rely on it to save him. He knew he was saved and justified by the blood of Jesus Christ alone.

But this phrase in Galatians 4:12 led some to question Paul's motives. It's similar to another statement he made in his letter to the Corinthian church: "I have become all things to all people, that by all means I might save some" (1 Corinthians 9:22 ESV). That's another phrase people within the church often use inappropriately; they fall back on the phrase to be "all things to all people" and use it as a ticket to do whatever they want because Paul did.

If someone becomes all things to all people, is that good or bad? Think of chameleons, animals that can change colors to become similar to objects around them. Chameleon believers become anything, even somebody who is manipulative, to be like others.

The Jews considered Paul a "Jew among Jews" who studied the *torah* under the best mentors. But to the gentiles, Paul seemed to be acting as if he was no longer under the law. Was this what it meant to "become all things to all people"?

Let's look at this passage and put it in context by examining a parallel passage in 1 Corinthians 9.

A Servant to All

> *For though I am free from all, I have made myself a servant to all, that I might win more of them. To the Jews I became as a Jew, in order to win the Jews. To those under the law I became as one under the law (though not being myself under the law) that I might win those under the law. To those outside the law I became as one outside the law (not being outside the law of God but under the law of Christ) that I might win those outside the law. To the weak I became weak, that I might win the weak. I have become all things to all people, that by all means I might save some.*
> *— 1 Corinthians 9:19 (ESV)*

Paul's ambition in becoming like those he was teaching was to serve, not to manipulate.

In his letter, he described how he was able to accomplish that task: "To the Jews I became as [like] a Jew, to win the Jews." How did Paul become a Jew? Did he have to do anything? No. He was not talking about his actions but his attitude.

He explained that when dealing with the people living under the law, he presented himself in the manner of someone under the law. But when dealing with gentiles, he presented himself with the attitude of someone not living under the law. But he added, "though I am not free from God's law" (1 Corinthians 9:21 NIV).

Paul pointed out that despite this apparent freedom of not being *under* the law, he was not *free* from the law. He knew he had limits and boundaries set by God.

At the end of Paul's life, when he was on trial before the Jews, he said, "I have never ceased to keep the Torah." Because of this, it is not accurate to say Paul became a chameleon to please everyone, because throughout 1 Corinthians 9 it is clear Paul set limits to whatever he did.

What was Paul's goal in preaching this message? He provided the answer in 1 Corinthians 9:22: "I have become all things to all people *so that by all possible means I might save some*" (NIV emphasis added). His goal was people's salvation.

He cared about the souls of the individuals to whom he was writing. He did not manipulate people to achieve their salvation, but came alongside people and showed he cared.

Earning Trust

Remember what happened when Paul went to Greece? Acts 17 reveals Paul watched the philosophers discussing things in the marketplace and observed that among the many idols there was an altar to an unknown god.

But Paul didn't jump in and say, "You guys are messed up! Look at all these foreign gods. You don't know what you're talking about! Let me tell you about Yahweh." Instead, he spoke tenderly and related to the Greeks by identifying their attempts at worship: "You have an altar to an unknown god. Let me tell you about Yahweh, because He is the God over all the others." That's what Paul meant when he said he became all things to all people. He started right where the person was.

People don't tend to trust others until they know they're friends and can be trusted.

Investing in Others

My wife sometimes calls me "the man with a thousand hobbies." I never really get good at any of them. I get to the point where I have some knowledge of them and then I move on to the next one. But one of the reasons why I've learned about so many different things is because I talk to people about their hobbies. And who isn't willing to talk about what interests them?

Similarly, Paul warned against sharing the gospel in a manipulative way. Believers should share the gospel because they care about an individual and they are willing to spend time with them.

Jesus was willing to spend time with those He wanted to disciple. He spent three years living with them and eating with them. He knew everything about them. This is what evangelism is supposed to look like: investing in another person by spending time with them out of love.

What Happened to Your Joy?

*Paul continued in Galatians 4 and said, "As you know, it was because of an illness that I first preached the gospel to you, and even though my illness was a trial to you, you did not treat me with contempt or scorn. Instead, you welcomed me as if I were an angel of God, as if I were Christ Jesus himself." — **Galatians 4:13 (NIV)***

When he first went to Galatia, he traveled up the mountain range and grew deathly sick. He was on a missionary journey to witness to the people of Galatia, but by the time he arrived he was half-dead.

Paul hadn't even had a chance to witness to them at that point, and yet they took him in and cared for him. They brought him back to health. Because of their hospitality he said, "You are people that I care deeply about because of how you've treated me. I care about your condition."

Then he asked, "What then has become of your blessedness?" (Galatians 4:15 ESV). "You were so full of joy when I was with you. Now you're letting these people tell you that you're not children of God unless you fully convert; you're letting them take away your joy."

Paul was fully invested in the Galatians; he cared deeply about their joy and their happiness—and ultimately, their salvation.

Labor Pains

Then Paul revealed what was really in his heart for these people. He began, "My dear children, for whom I am again in the pains of childbirth..." (Galatians 4:19 NIV). Why did Paul feel that way? Because he thought that they were fully convinced who Jesus was in their life, but realized he needed to address the issue again. He continued: "... how I wish I could be with you now and change my tone, because I am perplexed about you" (Galatians 4:20 NIV).

Metaphorically speaking, Paul was in childbirth. When a woman is pregnant, she knows she has about nine long months to wait before the baby is born. Childbirth is the moment every woman anticipates! Similarly, Paul was waiting expectantly for something, and often people assume he meant salvation, but is that what he intended to communicate? Look again at that verse. Paul said, "My dear children, for whom I am again in the pains of childbirth until Christ is formed in you." Paul was waiting for Christ to be fully formed in the Galatians, when they would be mature and developed in their faith.

But they're not there yet, and that's why he's said he had again found himself in the pains of childbirth. He was looking at their actions and thinking, "Have I done all of this for nothing?"

Becoming Disciples

Sometimes I'm asked why I don't do more invitations to receive Christ at church services. People assume it's because I don't care.

I absolutely do care. But what I care about is the same as Paul. I care about Christ being fully formed in an individual, because that is what brings light to the world—not somebody who stands up and makes a one-time commitment.

It is good to pray for a nation's government, leaders, and economy. But what is more important is to pray God's people become fully formed in Christ, because that's how the world is going to be affected. It's not going to be affected otherwise, because God does not violate the will of people. And it's the will of people that brings about much of the evil seen today.

Believers exist to disciple others. But that purpose can never be fulfilled until each believer is fully formed in them. They must become mature disciples in Christ before they can effectively disciple others.

It's easy to raise a hand, and even to walk forward, kneel at the altar, and make a commitment. But if that's the end of it, then the person has missed the whole boat. Paul was challenging Christians to seek to be fully formed in Christ. And that's a big difference.

The Marathon of Evangelism

Human beings tend to be goal-oriented, checking lists off to feel "finished." As followers of Christ, Paul said the believer's goal should be to invest in the lives of others.

When establishing goals in evangelism, sometimes Christians set their eyes on the wrong thing. Paul said the end goal is a fully discipled person. It's not a short game. It's not a sprint. It's a marathon.

I've sometimes had to work with people for years before they will step out and come with me to a Bible study. Sometimes I have to go hang out in bars with them before they know I'm not going to be judgmental and they can trust me. But in return they're willing to do things that I do.

That's friendship, isn't it? And that's what evangelism is.

Coming Back to the Goal

Paul's goal was not to manipulate; it was to befriend and serve. This is called lifestyle evangelism, becoming a friend to the person. It's starting exactly where they are.

Paul set limits right from the beginning. He said, "I want to become all things to all people, but this is what I'm going to do. My goal is to serve them out of my heart of love." Paul repeated this concept throughout his epistles. "Everything is permissible, but not everything is helpful" he said in 1 Corinthians 10:23 (HCSB). Not everything builds others up. Paul said he chose to do was profitable and what was meaningful.

People tend to reach a goal and then make a new one. Human goals tend to be easy, too superficial.

Unfortunately, that is what has happened within the church. Goals have been set so low that people miss the depth of what God wants to do in people's lives. It is critical that believers return to the true goal, to make disciples of all nations—starting with ourselves.

WORKBOOK

Chapter 10 Questions

Question: In what ways have you tried to be "all things to all people"? Were you simply serving them, or was there an aspect of manipulation? How can you be sure you are truly serving others, and not deceiving or being deceived, when you try to meet others on their terms?

_____

_____

_____

_____

_____

_____

_____

_____

_____

_____

_____

_____

Question: Where do you see a need for reconciliation in your life or in the Body of Christ? What steps can you take to initiate or further reconciliation within your sphere of influence?

_____

_____

_____

_____

_____

_____

_____

_____

_____

_____

_____

Question: What does evangelism based on discipleship and personal investment in others look like? What opportunities for such evangelism exist in your life now?

_____

_____

_____

_____

_____

_____

_____

_____

_____

_____

Action: Be "all things to people"—not to manipulate them, but to serve them in truth and love. Following Jesus' model, invest your time, energy, and care in others, building trust as the foundation of your relationship. Where you encounter offense, division, and resentment, follow His path of gentle, healing reconciliation. Thus, evangelize not only by sharing your faith and the message of the gospel, but above all by growing into a fully formed disciple of Christ and helping others do likewise—as the world looks on in amazement!

Chapter 10 Notes

CONCLUSION

Faith, Family, Freedom

One of the most crucial takeaways from the book of Galatians is that the law is not done away with. I know that's not what's being taught in the majority of churches, but Paul taught this concept over and over: the law has value.

In Romans 2:25–26 Paul wrote, "Circumcision indeed is of value if you obey the law, but if you break the law, your circumcision becomes uncircumcision. So, if a man who is uncircumcised keeps the precepts of the law, will not his uncircumcision be regarded as circumcision?" (ESV).

Circumcision was not about anything that happened in the flesh. Circumcision was about what people do; it was about obeying God. And Paul referred to this kind of circumcision as a circumcision of the heart.

In Romans 2:28 Paul said, "For no one is a Jew who is merely one outwardly, nor is circumcision outward or physical. But a Jew is one inwardly, and circumcision is a matter of the heart, by the Spirit, not by the letter. His praise is not from man but from God" (ESV).

The law simply cannot save a person. It takes a work of God, who makes a person into a new creation.

Part of Who We Are

Does that mean the law is gone and not needed anymore? Before Christ, the law revealed what disobedience was. In Christ, the law is still in the believer's life as a new creation, but has been transferred into their heart so they will *want* to obey God. It's not just an external rule to check off on the list, but part of who the believer is. Law and grace work together beautifully.

This is an act of the Spirit, which is what it means to be "circumcised of heart," and a new creation in Christ. It is a process that will take a lifetime, but one that each day makes a person more and more Christ-like.

Unity and Diversity

Understanding this concept—that the law and grace work together to lead us toward Christ—is paramount for the church. The belief that Christians have no responsibility to the law dulls the church's witness. Sadly, the church has begun to believe this lie and this has affected the Body of Christ. Followers of Jesus look the same as non-believers and live life however they see fit.

It is the law that makes Christians useful vessels for God, because the law is what sets people apart and makes them holy. How can the world see the light if believers are not living a life that reflects that light?

Jesus said, "When the Son of Man comes, will he find faith on the earth?" (Luke 18:8 ESV). He might see that the church has abandoned every word that God had spoken. And how tragic it would be if He returned and said, "I don't see faith."

Paul defined faith as a strong belief that causes a person to keep the law. It is a faith that makes people different, that changes them from the inside out. May the Lord return to find believers trusting in His Word and teaching others to do the same!

Freedom to Be Different

Though we must be one in faith, love, and ultimate purpose, Christians also have to let each other be different if that's the way God has created them. And sometimes, they might even need to be encouraged to be different.

Christians should have the freedom to be who God created them to be—different from each other, unique and perfectly designed for the particular purpose for which He has created them. As children in a natural family are diverse in gender, personality, and interests, so are the children of God.

It's time for the church to remember the main theme of Paul's message to the Galatians: unity. Anyone who believes in Jesus is a child of God and part of His family—a family united in faith, obedience, and purpose.

Notes

1. "Judaizers." From *Baker's Evangelical Dictionary of Biblical Theology Online*. *Bible Study Tools*. http://www.biblestudytools.com/dictionaries/bakers-evangelical-dictionary/judaizers.html
2. "Phroureo." The KJV New Testament Greek Lexicon. *Bible Study Tools*. http://www.biblestudytools.com/lexicons/greek/kjv/phroureo.html
3. Smith, Malcolm. *The Lost Secret of the New Covenant*. Harrison House, 2002, p. 12–13.
4. "Strong's H4940—mishpachah." *Blue Letter Bible*. https://www.blueletterbible.org/lang/lexicon/lexicon.cfm?Strongs=H4940&t=KJV
5. Warren Wiersbe. *Be Right*. In *The BE Series Bundle: Paul's Letters*. David C. Cook, 2015.
6. "Romans 4:1–3 Commentary." *Precept Austin*. http://www.preceptaustin.org/romans_41-3
7. "Redeem." Merriam-Webster, 2016. http://www.merriam-webster.com/dictionary/redeem

8. "Strong's H2617—checed." *Blue Letter Bible.* https://www.blueletterbible.org/lang/lexicon/lexi con.cfm?t=kjv&strongs=h2617

9. Yee, Chua Siang. "Mystery Marathon 'Winner' Just Wanted T-shirt and Medal." *The Straits Times.* 19 Jan. 2016. http://www.straitstimes.com/sport/mystery-marathon-winner-just-wanted-t-shirt-and-medal

10. "4150 moed." From *NAS Exhaustive Concordance of the Bible with Hebrew-Aramaic and Greek Dictionaries*, 1998, The Lockman Foundation. *BibleHub.* http://biblehub.com/hebrew/4150.htm

11. "John Wesley." Bible.org. https://bible.org/illustration/john-wesley-0

12. Moen, Skip. "Different Strokes." *Hebrew Word Study.* http://skipmoen.com/2016/03/different-strokes/

13. Courson, Jon. *Courson's Application Commentary, New Testament.* Thomas Nelson, 2003.

REFERENCES

Bibliography

Eisenbaum, Pamela. *Paul was Not a Christian: The Original Message of a Misunderstood Apostle.* HarperOne 2010.

Janicki, Toby. *God-Fearers: Gentiles and the God of Israelites.* Marshfield, MO: First Fruits of Zion, 2012.

Lancaster, D. Thomas. *The Holy Epistle to the Galatians.* Marshfield, MO: First Fruits of Zion, 2014.

Nanos, Mark. The Irony of Galatians: Paul Letter in First Century Context. Minneapolis, MN: Fortress Press, 1996.

Moen, Skip. Ph.D. *Spiritual Restoration Volume I.* 2008.

Young, H. Brad. *Meet the Rabbis: Rabbinic Thought and the Teachings of Jesus.* Grand Rapids, MI: Baker Academic, 2007.

About the Author

Dr. Christopher Leonard is currently pastor of
Community Church of Fish Creek, Wisconsin, in Door
County. Dr. Leonard has a B.A. from Crown College, a
Masters of Divinity and a Doctor of Biblical Studies for
Master International University of Divinity. He has been
married to Kris Ann for 36 years and has three children,
Aaron, Tara, and Torry.

About Sermon To Book

SermonToBook.com began with a simple belief: that sermons should be touching lives, *not* collecting dust. That's why we turn sermons into high-quality books that are accessible to people all over the globe.

Turning your sermon series into a book exposes more people to God's Word, better equips you for counseling, accelerates future sermon prep, adds credibility to your ministry, and even helps make ends meet during tight times.

John 21:25 tells us that the world itself couldn't contain the books that would be written about the work of Jesus Christ. Our mission is to try anyway. Because, in Heaven, there will no longer be a need for sermons or books. Our time is now.

If God so leads you, we'd love to work with you on your sermon or sermon series.

Visit www.sermontobook.com to learn more.